DATE DUE

FE 22 '97		
FE 17 '97		
FE 08 '03		
FE 8 '03		

Politics
and Social
Welfare Policy
in the
United States

Politics
and Social
Welfare Policy
in the
United States

Robert X Browning

The University of Tennessee Press / Knoxville

Library of Congress Cataloging-in-Publication Data

Browning, Robert X, 1950–
  Politics and social welfare policy in the United States.

  Bibliography: p.
  Includes index.
  1. United States—Social policy. 2. Social
service—United States—History—20th century.
3. United States—Politics and government—1945–
4. United States—Economic conditions—1945–
5. Federal aid to public welfare—United States—
History—20th century. I. Title.
HV95.B73 1986   361.6'0973   85-17837
ISBN 0-87049-486-4 (alk. paper)

To my parents

Contents

Tables and Figures

TABLES

Acknowledgments

This book has evolved from an idea in an early graduate research seminar and a later thesis. Over this period there have been refinements, revisions, and much reanalysis, and many people have helped to shape and hone my ideas and analyses. Barbara Hinckley constantly reminded me of the importance of trying to measure the impact of political institutions on policy; she read the manuscript through countless drafts in many stages of this research. Ira Sharkansky provided numerous insights and encouragements through our conversations about this project.

Others who gave valuable advice and comments include Sheldon Danziger, Jack Dennis, James Donoghue, Thomas Hammond, Diane Kaiser, Gary King, Bert Kritzer, Robert Lampman, Ben Page, Robert Plotnick, Lyn Ragsdale, and Syl Schieber. Richard Winters, Rod Kiewiet, Aaron Wildavsky, and William McLauchlan read the manuscript and provided useful comments and suggestions.

Susan Anderson and Seung-Hyun Kim gave invaluable research help. Assistance was made available by the Institute for Research on Poverty at the University of Wisconsin, Purdue Research Foundation, the Center for Public Policy and Administration at Purdue University, and the Dirksen Center for Congressional Studies. The data analysis was facilitated through the assistance of the staff of the Data and Program Library Service at the University of Wisconsin and Bernard Dugoni at Purdue University. Alma McMillan and Ann Bixby of the Social Security Administration and Robert Plotnick provided data used in the analysis.

I was fortunate to have two editors at the University of Tennessee Press, Mavis Bryant and Cynthia Maude-Gembler, whose interest and advice was invaluable at each step of the way. Katherine Holloway's editing improved the manuscript immensely. I would also like to thank the faculty and staff at the University of Wisconsin and Purdue University who provided assistance of various kinds. David Caputo and William Shaffer were particularly helpful. Beth Henschen provided encouragement and friendship whenever needed. Throughout, my family has been supportive and encouraging as well. Most especially, I wish to thank my parents and my brothers and sisters for all the help they have given.

I

Themes and Characteristics
of Social Welfare Policy

Perhaps no government policy has as many fervent supporters and detractors as does social welfare policy in the United States. To supporters, social programs represent the positive contribution of the government to provide the basic necessities of food, housing, and health care to the needy; to provide income payments to the retired, the disabled, and the unemployed; and to invest in human capital through education, training, and employment programs. To detractors of the welfare state, these social programs are variously seen as unnecessary government intervention, as failed programs which discourage initiative and encourage dependence, and as costly programs which are beyond government budgetary control. Although there has been widespread support for programs such as social security and veterans' benefits, the debate over the shape and size of social programs has occurred in every Congress and in every administration since the inception of the programs.

While social programs in the United States have their origins in the New Deal period, the major growth and expansion has occurred since the Second World War. In the decade from 1935 to 1945, the federal government spent less than $4 billion on all social programs.[1] This amount more than doubled in the next ten years and increased twelve times between 1960 and 1980.

From 1950 to 1964, expenditures for social welfare comprised less than 30 percent of all federal expenditures. In 1980, social welfare expenditures were 54 percent of all federal expenditures.

Much has been written about U.S. social programs. Political scientists have chronicled the enactment and modification of every program.[2] Alternatives to current programs have been proposed, analyzed, and debated by political scientists, policy analysts, and economists.[3] A great deal is also known about who benefits from these social programs.[4] Despite all of these research efforts, a major gap in our understanding remains. While much is known about particular programs, very little in any systematic way is known about how changes in social programs have resulted from political control of our national government.[5]

This book examines the political and economic factors that have affected the growth and the shape of federal social programs in the post-Second World War period. The approach here differs from previous analyses of social welfare policy in two ways. First, this study considers the broad range of U.S. programs. It does not focus on a single program or a set of programs such as health or education. In order to avoid the endless detail and descriptions of individual program differences, summary measures of expenditures which are comparable across programs are employed. In addition, where possible, measures of benefit levels, indicators of program eligibility, summaries of conditions of assistance, and indicators of the federal share of program contributions are used. These measures of policy permit comparisons across programs. Thus the analysis allows linkages to the political factors that affect benefits as well as to the impact of these benefit programs on the targeted groups.

This book has a second equally important component. Using summary program measures, the analysis indicates how changes in program growth, amount, and targeting of benefits have resulted from political control of the national government interacting with economic conditions. The influence of the party of the president, the party margins in the Congress, the differing congressional committee jurisdictions over social programs, and the rhythm of the political calendar are observed as effects on the summary indicators of U.S. social programs. The analysis thus links the study of public policy with the study of political institutions to describe and analyze the effect of our political process on the outcomes of that process.

In this chapter the characteristics of U.S. social programs, which have been noted and usually lamented in previous studies, are described. These characteristics include the diversity, the categorical nature, the fragmentation, and the increased role of the federal government. The second chapter, in particular, shows how these characteristics result from policy choices made by the president and the Congress influenced by economic conditions, previous decisions, and the political calendar.

THE DIVERSITY OF U.S. SOCIAL WELFARE PROGRAMS

In this study reliance is placed on the definition of social welfare expenditures long used by the Social Security Administration. These are cash and noncash programs which "are of direct benefit to individuals. Included are cash benefit programs for income maintenance through social insurance and public aid, and those providing in-kind support through health, education, housing, and other welfare services."[6] The noncash programs are commonly referred to as in-kind because they include services or reimbursement to providers rather than cash payments to individuals. Cash payments allow the recipients discretion to spend the money as they choose. In-kind assistance directs the benefit toward a particular need such as food, housing, or education.

U.S. social programs include over 170 programs paying $300 billion of benefits to 40 million households. The programs range from the largest, social security retirement, to one of the smallest, the Indian Health Scholarship program. Most federal programs have their origin in the New Deal. Before that time, social welfare was a mix of state, local, and private efforts. While the role of the federal government has vastly changed and the size of the present federal programs dwarfs the modest New Deal beginnings, the basic shape and character of present-day programs still reflect much of the New Deal origin.

The Social Security Act of 1935 signed by President Franklin D. Roosevelt contained provisions for Old Age Insurance; unemployment compensation; assistance to the needy who were aged, who were blind, or who had dependent children.[7] It also provided for child welfare and maternal and child health services. Since that time, health and disability insurance have been added. Benefit coverage has been expanded to widows, spouses, children, and students. Today benefits paid under the provisions of the Social Security Act constitute 58 percent of all U.S. federal social welfare expenditures and 31 percent of the total U.S. federal expenditures.

Beyond the social insurance programs, federal program expansion has been of in-kind expenditures. These include expenditures for food, housing, education, and training programs. Few new cash programs have been enacted since the New Deal. The new program enactments since 1940 have been of in-kind rather than cash programs. In-kind expenditures as a percent of total expenditures steadily declined from 35 percent in 1949 to 7 percent in the late fifties as veterans' benefit programs declined in participation. This percentage rose again rapidly in the early to mid-1960s, however, as Democratic congresses enacted new social service and Great Society programs. By 1977, in-kind expenditures constituted 38 percent of total federal social welfare spending, reflecting ever increasing expenditures for health and food programs.

THE CATEGORICAL NATURE OF U.S. PROGRAMS

The underlying program diversity is reflected in the categorical nature of U.S. social programs which in turn is a function of the political philosophies which shaped the programs at their creation. The original Social Security Act provided assistance payments to needy individuals who fell into three categories. To be eligible one had to be aged, blind, or a dependent child whose parents were either dead or could not provide adequate assistance. Additional categories made eligible for public assistance included the disabled and the families of dependent children.

A similar pattern of expansion can be seen in the insurance provisions of the Social Security Act. Widows, spouses, children, and disabled workers were made eligible to receive all or part of the insured worker's benefit. Health benefits were made available in a limited way first for the public assistance categories, then for the insured categories (Medicare), and at the same time expanded in a broader program for the poor (Medicaid).

Each enactment of in-kind benefit programs set conditions for program eligibility. These might be income level, family characteristics, or medical conditions. All of these provisions reflected a basic American philosophy. Part of that philosophy held that benefits should be earned through work. This social insurance concept is reflected in the provisions of the Social Security Act. A person who can no longer work because of age or disability is entitled to some portion of his earnings as a benefit. Spouses, widows, and children were later entitled to share in a portion of the primary worker's benefit. Social security retirement and survivor benefits, disability benefits, health benefits, and unemployment benefits all are social insurance programs.

A second part of the American philosophy reflected in the design of our social programs concerns government payments made as a last resort to those people who cannot work. This philosophy extends the concept of the Elizabethan poor laws in which public charity is available to the downtrodden but is never seen as a desirable substitute for work.[8] The public assistance programs are federal-state programs in which levels of benefits vary widely from state to state.

The philosophy of the American work ethic is also seen in the

more favorable consideration given to the provisions and beneficiaries of the Social Security Act than to those of the public
assistance programs. Even with the public assistance and in-
kind benefit provisions, some categories of beneficiaries are
more favored than others. The "truly needy"—defined as the
aged, the infirm, the disabled—have realized more benefits than
other groups. Veterans and children are also considered to be
groups afforded special consideration. A second way in which
this work ethic is manifest is in the willingness of Congress to
provide in-kind benefits rather than cash to those who can
work. This stems in part from a fear that the poor will squander
their money rather than spend it wisely on essential needs such
as food, shelter, and health care. Throughout the book these
considerations are seen in the patterns of the targeting of assistance programs and in the provision of in-kind programs.

THE ABSENCE OF A COMPREHENSIVE APPROACH

One consequence of the categorical nature of U.S. programs is
that some beneficiary groups are favored while others are not.[9]
Our fragmented, myriad system of programs may actually lead
to situations in which some persons are ineligible for benefits.
For groups such as veterans, there are special welfare provisions
for the poor. The cause of a veteran's poverty may be no different
from that of another individual—that is, it is not necessarily a
consequence of military service. The other individual, because
he or she is not a veteran, must find eligibility in another category. That category may carry the connotation of "welfare," while
the veteran's welfare benefit is termed a "pension."

The consequences of the varied treatment of categories of
eligible beneficiaries are seen most clearly in the numbers of
pre-transfer and post-transfer poor. In 1965, 21.3 percent of the
population were considered in poverty by the measure of
pre-transfer income[10]—that is, they were in poverty before re-

ceiving any government cash and in-kind benefits. When one considers post-transfer income—income after government benefits—15.6 percent were still in poverty in 1965. By 1978, these figures show 20.2 percent in pre-transfer poverty and 11.4 percent in post-transfer poverty. Considering a third indicator of post-transfer poverty, the progress against poverty appears more striking. Adjusted income counts all in-kind benefits as well as cash benefits, corrects for underreporting of income, and measures income after taxes. Adjusted income poverty figures show 12.1 percent remaining in poverty in 1965. By 1978, only 5.9 percent remain in poverty after receiving government assistance.

The cash transfer payments have by and large lifted the aged from poverty. The pre- and post-transfer rate for the aged is higher than that of the population as a whole. This was true in 1965 and is true in 1978. These figures, however, mask the tremendous progress made against poverty among the aged from 1969 to 1974. During this period the percent of aged in post-transfer poverty fell 2 percent a year, twice the annual decrease observed in the previous ten-year period. Since 1974, the post-transfer rate of the aged poor has "remained virtually stagnant" at between 14 and 16 percent.[11] The gains of the nonelderly during this period were much lower and in 1980–81 shifted upward much more sharply than did the percent of the elderly in poverty.

The same progress cannot be seen with the working poor. The latter are those who are in poverty by consequence of the fact that they work in low-paying jobs or have large families. There are few transfer programs for these individuals. They may be eligible for some food, housing, or health benefits. If the number of persons poor after transfers is noted, it is found that the working poor are disproportionately represented. Many of these persons may refuse benefits because they eschew "welfare." At the same time, providing assistance without stigma to the aged or the veterans perpetuates this myth of the deserving and undeserving poor.

7

This absence of a comprehensive approach to U.S. social welfare policy was described in 1972 by a staff study for the Congressional Joint Economic Committee.

> In general an incremental approach has been followed, but it is no longer possible—if, indeed, it ever was—to provide a convincing rationale for the programs as they exist in terms of who is covered and who is excluded, benefit amounts, and eligibility conditions. No coherent rationale binds them together as a system. Additionally, the programs are extraordinarily complex, and the eligibility conditions and entitlement provisions lack uniformity even among programs with similar objectives and structures. Public retirement programs, for example, differ widely in their generosity to covered workers. And, a number of the income-tested programs reach the same part of the population but have been developed separately without apparent consistency of objectives, operating features, and equity.[12]

The incremental approach made program expansion possible as additional benefits or additional beneficiary groups were added to existing programs. The fragmented, incremental picture mirrors the policy orientation of the Congress with jurisdiction over programs divided among numerous committees—each with their own constituency, goals, and history. In sum, those who study the political system and policy making would not find this surprising but instead see this fragmentation and the varying patterns of growth as the phenomena to be explained.

Many have criticized our fragmented system and advocated comprehensive reforms through refundable tax credits or a guaranteed income.[13] The approach here is not to join in this debate. Instead the analysis seeks to show how this fragmentation has been fostered by our political system. Furthermore, we examine the course and trends in the adjustment, expansion, and targeting of benefits. In this way we can better understand how our present system has developed and the consequences in terms of who benefits and the distribution of income.

THE EXPANSION OF FEDERAL PROGRAMS

Since the New Deal the role of the government in providing for social welfare has gradually shifted from the state and local governments to the federal government. National concerns about equalizing benefits among states, and efforts to prod states to increase social spending have been achieved through the "federalization" of many formerly state programs. In some cases, state programs have been made federal programs. The 1973 enactment of Supplemental Security Income (SSI) was such a program change. In other cases the federal government has increased its program contribution as an incentive to states to increase benefits or otherwise reform state programs.

The changing role of the state and federal government is seen in the ratio of federal to state spending for social programs. The figures in Table 1-1 indicate that in 1950 the federal government spent 86 cents for every dollar spent on social welfare by state and local governments. In 1980, the federal government was spending $1.60 for each state and local dollar. Federal expenditures increased thirty fold during this period, while state and local expenditures increased by a factor of fifteen. The patterns and pressures for this federal program growth will be examined in more detail in subsequent chapters.

TABLE 1-1
State–Federal Social Welfare Comparisons
(in millions of nominal dollars)[1]

	FY1950	FY1960	FY1970	FY1980
Federal	$10,541	$24,882	$77,077	$303,345
State	12,200	25,200	63,100	190,010
Ratio[2]	0.86	0.99	1.22	1.60

[1] Figures include administrative expenses.

[2] Ratio of federal to state expenditures.

Source: *Social Security Bulletin. Annual Statistical Supplement, 1977–79,* p. 53. Washington, D.C., Government Printing Office. Ann Kallman Bixby, "Social Welfare Expenditures, Fiscal Year 1980," *Social Security Bulletin* 46 (Aug. 1983): 9–17.

DIFFERENTIAL RATES OF PROGRAM GROWTH

While the themes of diversity, categorical eligibility, fragmentation, and federal expansion are observed throughout the history of U.S. social programs, the rates of program growth have varied tremendously. These different program growth rates are the result of the different emphases which have been placed on social policy by Congress and the president over time. During the 1950s the growth was in cash programs—primarily social security and public assistance. In the 1960s under the Kennedy and Johnson administrations, in-kind expenditures—education, social services, and health—were the dominant growth areas. In the late 60s and early 70s under the Nixon and Ford administrations, food stamps and manpower programs grew rapidly with a resurgence of growth in cash programs. Health continued to grow because of the enactment of previous laws. Table 1-2 shows the pattern of some of these changes.

Since many political science and policy studies have focused on the Great Society programs, there is a commonly held view

TABLE 1-2

Federal Social Welfare Expenditures by Category (in millions of nominal dollars)

	FY1950	FY1960	FY1970	FY1980
Social Insurance	$2,103.0	$14.307.2	$45,245.6	$191,106.9
Public Assistance	1,103.2	2,116.9	9,648.6	49,252.2
Veterans	6,386.2	5,367.3	8,951.5	21,253.6
Education	156.7	867.9	5,875.8	12,990.2
Health and Medical	603.5	1,737.1	4,775.2	13,348.0
Housing	14.6	143.5	581.6	6,608.1
Other	174.0	416.7	2,258.9	8,785.9
Total	$10,541.2	$24.956.6	$77,337.2	$303,344.9

Source: "Social Welfare Expenditures, Fiscal Year 1978." Alma W. McMillan and Ann Kallman Bixby, *Social Security Bulletin* 43 (May 1980):3–17. Ann Kallman Bixby, "Social Welfare Expenditures, Fiscal Year 1980," *Social Security Bulletin* 46 (Aug. 1983):9–17.

that these programs gave rise to large increases in social welfare expenditures. While the Johnson administration initiatives were innovative in their attempt to deliver social services, the original War on Poverty programs were not major spending programs. The costly initiatives in the Johnson years were the Medicare and the Elementary and Secondary Education Acts. The analysis in subsequent chapters will show that some of the most costly and extensive increases came in the early Nixon administration. The Johnson War on Poverty did, however, elevate the problem of poverty to a prominent position on the national agenda. "What does it do for the poor?" became a question asked of all domestic programs.[14]

Another result of these different program emphases across time has been the change in the relative share of programs. As Table 1-3 reveals, the percent of total federal dollars spent on social insurance increased over the last three decades from 20 percent to over 60 percent, while veterans expenditures moved exactly in the opposite direction. All the other program categories show increases in the share of the total except health. While there have been very large increases within these categories the

TABLE 1-3
Federal Social Welfare Expenditures by Category as Percent of Total

	FY1950	FY1960	FY1970	FY1980
Social Insurance	20.0%	57.3%	58.5%	63.0%
Public Assistance	10.5	8.5	12.5	16.2
Veterans	60.6	21.5	11.6	7.0
Education	1.5	3.5	7.6	4.3
Health and Medical	5.7	7.0	6.2	4.4
Housing	0.1	0.6	1.0	2.2
Other	1.6	1.7	2.9	2.9
Total	100 %	100 %	100 %	100 %

Source: Alma W. McMillan and Ann Kallman Bixby, "Social Welfare Expenditures, Fiscal Year 1978," *Social Security Bulletin* 43 (May 1980):3–17. Ann Kallman Bixby, "Social Welfare Expenditures, Fiscal Year 1980," *Social Security Bulletin* 46 (Aug. 1983):9–17.

absolute size of the expenditures for social insurance dwarf the other categories.

The election of Ronald Reagan brought a new era to spending for social programs at the federal level. President Reagan was committed to scaling down the federal social welfare effort and to achieve budget savings through reductions in entitlement programs. The changes brought about by Reagan can be more fully understood once the earlier periods and direction of expansion are analyzed.

POLITICS AND SOCIAL POLICY

The policy differences set forth, the program categories described, the different rates of growth alluded to in this book all provide the framework for analyzing social welfare policy. The purpose of this discussion is to illustrate the comparisons which will be made across programs. Providing these comparisons, however, is but a part of this analysis. Subsequent chapters will show how shifts in program expenditures, enactments of new programs, expansion of eligibility, or increases in federal program contribution result from political factors. Previous analyses of social welfare policy have told much about the politics of single programs or, alternatively, much about groups of programs, but little about the politics. Studies of Congress and the presidency have taught much about the behavior of these two bodies, but little about their effect on policy. In this analysis, a synthesis and integration—a synthesis of the varied social policies and an integration of the political causes with these policies—will be the goal.

In the next chapter some of the political and economic influences on social welfare policy are discussed. In chapter three the problems of measuring social policy are outlined. Specific programs within the categories of social welfare expenditures are detailed in chapter four. In subsequent chapters the effect of political and economic influences on the measures of social welfare policy are analyzed. These include decisions to increase benefits, to modify conditions of assistance, or to change the federal program share. Finally, the overall effect of these political factors on the design and impact of U.S. social programs are examined. The reader ought not expect to find a "coherent rationale" that binds these programs together but rather seek to understand how our political system, interacting with economic events, has resulted in the pattern of programs and benefits.

2

Politics and
Social Policy

To understand how political factors have affected U.S. social welfare policies requires a synthesis of several perspectives. The difficulty of this synthesis stems from the different orientations of the fields of political science, each of which have addressed the questions of policy influences. From the studies of Congress and the presidency, explanations of when and how these institutions have affected policy may be drawn upon. Additional explanations are derived from studies of the policy making process and from studies of the making of particular policies. Finally, the policy studies are relied upon to develop measures of policy which can be linked to political institutions.

Previous studies of U.S. social policy have emphasized but one of these perspectives. Some have analyzed the congressional and presidential influences without understanding the policies. Other studies describe the policies in great detail and indicate the ins and outs of the process but do not fully consider the findings of the empirical literature on Congress and the presidency. On the one hand, institutional scholars know about the Congress and the presidency, but not about policy. On the other hand, policy scholars know about policy, but not about the political institutions. In this analysis explanations about policy influence gleaned from the literature on Congress and the presidency are pulled together and linked to a particular policy area which has been influenced by these political institutions.

The intent here is to try to show explicitly what effect differences in political control of the national government have on spending for federal social programs in the post-war period. Do elections make a difference? Do presidents or Congress influence spending decisions? Do differences in party control of the presidency and the Congress influence spending levels? What are the relationships of political control, economic conditions, and social spending? Have certain types of social programs been favored over others by presidents of different parties?

Social welfare policy encompasses a large class of policies with differing conditions, target groups, and periods of growth. These policies have been marked by party differences and controversy. They are designed to provide income protection under adverse economic conditions and are thus responsive to these conditions. Social benefits are also subject to manipulation by elected officials who seek to gain favor with the electorate at opportune times. Finally, the noncomprehensive policy process is seen in the categorical nature and shared responsibility for federal social welfare policy.

These questions can be addressed through an examination of the empirical literature on the Congress and the presidency. From this literature five explanations for influences on policy can be drawn. These are general explanations which will be stated and explored more specifically throughout the book. These policy influences can be stated as follows.

1. *Decisions of political actors.* These are recommendations of the president or decisions of the Congress to increase benefits or to otherwise affect the conditions of assistance or program characteristics.

2. *Changes in economic conditions.* Specifically, these economic conditions are changes in unemployment or increases in prices. It is necessary to distinguish and separate those effects

which result automatically in response to economic conditions and those which result from decisions of political actors. The political decisions may be triggered by changes in economic conditions.

3. *Cyclical regularities in the political calendar.* Specifically, these are the occurrence of elections and the beginning of new presidential terms. The presidential "honeymoon" has long been described as a period conducive to policy changes. The electoral cycle is a more recent explanation of changes in social welfare programs.

4. *Previous decisions of political actors.* The incremental model of policy making is dominant throughout explanations of American policy. Rather than examining and enacting comprehensive policy reforms, policy makers consider only a limited set of alternatives and make small adjustments to existing policies. For social welfare policy an analysis of the extent to which current expenditures result from decisions made by current policy makers or from decisions made in previous congresses can be explored.

5. *Differing congressional committee jurisdictions.* Congressional studies have long suggested that committee differences give rise to policy differences. Similarly, policy case accounts invariably suggest that committee membership change or leadership change was important in the enactment of particular programs. Since social welfare programs fall under the jurisdiction of about a dozen House and Senate committees, one might expect that committee jurisdiction would have an effect on social welfare programs.

DECISIONS OF POLITICAL ACTORS

The Majority Party in Congress

Two macrolevel explanations of political influences on policy can be derived from the literature on Congress and the presidency. The first stems from the majority party control of Congress; the second from the relationship of the presidency and Congress. Evidence of party voting and divergent party positions on social issues support the argument that partisan margins in Congress ought to have policy effects. Support for social welfare programs has been a part of Democratic party platforms since the 1950s and is seen in party cleavages on roll call votes of social issues in Congress.[1]

American political parties, while often viewed as weak links between the public and the government, nonetheless have important functions and differences which may affect policy. First, we are interested in political parties not as independent political institutions, but in parties in Congress and the party of the president. Political parties in Congress serve an organizing and leadership function which can be viewed as distinct from other party functions.[2] Parties in Congress choose the committee members and chairpersons, elect the speaker, and use the party based leadership organization to enforce some semblance of party voting. Second, American political parties, while not ideologically distinct, have differed on one dimension fundamental to the policies analyzed here. The Democratic party has traditionally favored a larger government role in providing for social welfare and economic intervention than has the Republican party. Sorauf terms these the "silent ideologies" of the American parties.[3] Finally, the influence of political parties on policy through the institutions of Congress and the presidency has not been fully explored empirically. There is ample evidence of the occurrences of party voting and party positions for different policy categories. What is not known is whether and how these party differences affect policy.

Earlier studies of roll call voting indicate that there are party cleavages on voting for social issues. For example, Clausen finds that party cohesion was strong for the Republicans on both social welfare and government management dimensions and slightly weaker for the Democrats for the 83rd to 88th Congresses.[4] Adopting Clausen's methodology, Sinclair sees social welfare emerging as part of a major political agenda in the 71st Congress (1929–30).[5] Voting on social welfare policy began in a partisan fashion and continued so well into the 1930s.

Evidence of party voting and divergent party positions on social issues lead to the conclusion that partisan margins in Congress should have policy effects. Case studies of policy enactments following the election of 1948 and 1964 also support this contention.[6] Sundquist details the policy role of the liberal Democrats from 1952 to 1960 and their subsequent role when the Democrats took control of the presidency in 1961.[7] Although the Democrats were in control of both houses and the presidency in 1961, the five-vote margin on the procedural motion to expand the Rules Committee was an indication of the tenuous nature of the majority. Ripley has further differentiated types of congressional majorities based on partisan control of the presidency and Congress.[8] He suggests that policy success of the parties will depend upon combinations of presidential and congressional party control.

Additional evidence of the influence of partisan majorities is found in a study by Bozeman. In an analysis of appropriations for forty-two agencies from 1950 to 1971, he finds that HEW appropriations are most directly related to social welfare expenditures and that "appropriation rates for HEW agencies rise in periods of economic decline and with increases in partisan strength for the Democratic party, but the effect of the economic and partisan variables is largely independent."[9]

A further indication of the importance of the Democratic majority in influencing appropriations is presented by Davis, Dempster, and Wildavsky. In an effort to explain nonincremental exceptions and exogenous influences to their basic model of the appropriations process, they find that Democrats support a higher level of spending than Republicans.[10] This is consistent with the findings of other studies and with previous findings of appropriation studies that the Senate tends to support a higher level of spending than the House.

Region and Ideology

This relationship between the Democratic majority and social spending can be further explored by considering regional and ideological differences within the Democratic party. While congressional studies still find that party is a major predictor of roll call voting, region and constituency characteristics are also important. On social welfare issues, partisan voting by southern Democrats has been much lower than that of their northern Democratic colleagues. Clausen finds low support for social welfare issues among a majority of southern Democrats, but high support among northern Democrats.[11] Sinclair pinpoints the 79th Congress (1945–46) as the time when this pattern was established.[12]

The regional distinction between northern and southern Democrats is used extensively as a proxy for ideology. Although Clausen does use a measure of ideology created from roll call votes, he admits that "The three-way division (northern Democrats, southern Democrats, and Republicans) not only represents geography and party, but is a convenient way to describe politicians in terms of the mix of party and ideology."[13] Cooper and Bombardier find that the much heralded success of the 89th Congress (1965–66) is attributable to the influx of northern freshman Democrats whose level of partisan support compensated for declining partisan support among southern Democrats.[14] Hinckley has argued that the party voting in this 89th Congress had consequences for Conservative Coalition activity and declining southern Democratic support in subsequent Congresses.[15]

Despite this evidence of party differences on social welfare policy, there has been a convergence as well. This convergence is seen in case accounts of presidential policy positions on different types of social welfare policy. It is obscured by the congressional roll call indicators of social welfare policy which mask differences among categories and beneficiary groups within social welfare policy. President Eisenhower's support for expansion of social insurance programs while recommending a smaller federal role in public assistance programs is a case in point. The similarities of congressional and presidential positions on social insurance programs across presidencies also illustrate this point. The classification of social welfare by policy type and beneficiary group permits the analysis of hypotheses about the convergence of parties on social welfare policy as well as the exploration of differences in the institutional policy posture of the president and Congress, which are based not on party but on norms and roles of the respective institutions. That is, does the president's role in balancing the budget lead to support for programs which favor low income groups while Congress supports programs which distribute benefits more broadly across income groups and constituencies? These hypotheses are supported by the congressional literature which emphasizes congressional concern for reelection over party influences.[16]

The number of nonsouthern Democrats elected to the House needs to be considered as a factor which influences levels of spending for U.S. social programs. This regional classification measures both constituency and ideology and is well established in the congressional literature as a subclassification for party voting. It is expected to affect the committee membership and the number of southern and northern Republican votes needed to pass new legislation or modify existing programs.

Congress and the Presidency

Another thrust of the policy and institutions research has focused on the influence of the presidency. Much of the case literature has been dominated by presidential explanations which emphasize the president as the initiator and innovator in the policy process. Schattschneider argues that American government is presidential government in which a plebiscitary president is given mandate to govern.[17] Additionally, the policy literature has long been presidentially oriented. The president, as the most visible, public leader, must prod, cajole, and otherwise entice a reluctant Congress to enact presidential proposals.[18] Contributing to this image of policy dominance is control of information, the election by a nationwide constituency, a longer term in office than representatives, plus all of the institutional advantages, foremost of which is the ability to dominate the news which come with the office of the president.[19] Charles Lindblom's observation in a policy text is fairly typical of this theme.[20]

> As government takes on new functions over the years, some of them like monetary management, foreign aid, and space exploration, pose problems beyond the competence and time that Congress can bring to their solution . . . roughly eighty percent of the bills enacted into law now originate in the executive branch; and the President now largely determines the policy-making agenda of Congress, although less so than a British prime minister or cabinet does for Parliament.

The themes of the congressional reform literature also contribute to the dominance of the image of the president as policy innovator. Huntington typifies this sentiment in an essay on congressional limitations: "The congressional role in legislation has largely been reduced to delay and amendment."[21] He recommends that Congress emphasize its oversight role which it is institutionally more capable of handling. The perception that the president is the initiator and innovator in the policy process has been ingrained in much of the policy literature but is an overstatement that has overshadowed the few efforts to establish how that dominance varies across presidencies and parties and with the partisan composition of Congress.

There are only a few studies which have gone beyond the analysis of single policy cases. These include Sundquist's study of policy making in the Eisenhower, Kennedy and Johnson administrations.[22] Orfield studies congressional policy initiatives in a later era.[23] Light has utilized Domestic Council data to compare policy initiatives of presidents from Kennedy to Carter.[24] Others have used summary indicators such as presidential success scores or party support scores.[25] These provide a comparison of presidential activity and success, but not of the policy effect of this success.

Presidential Party or Presidential Cycles

Partisan control of the presidency may affect policy outcomes. The arguments for these effects are similar to those for the influence of the majority party in Congress. Again the empirical evidence is scant. Hibbs has demonstrated four-year cycles in unemployment corresponding to partisan control of the presidency. "Democratic administrations engineer downward movements in the U.S. unemployment level, whereas the reverse is true of Republican administrations," he concludes.[26] This is an important finding which shows the effect of partisan control of the presidency on macroeconomic policy. A recent analysis by Beck qualifies this finding by showing that the size of the party effect is only half the size of Hibbs's estimate (1.24 percent versus 2.36 percent) and that unemployment actually increased during some Democratic administrations.[27] Beck suggests that policies and coalitions which affect party positions vary by presidencies. One needs to look at administrations separately, he argues, rather than assume that presidents of the same party have the same macroeconomic policy interests. This debate over administration versus party effects is far from resolved.[28]

Tufte provides some evidence that political control of the economy follows an election cycle.[29] That is, administrations seek to lower unemployment and increase transfer benefits on a two-year cycle corresponding to elections. Although the Eisenhower years are a notable exception, Tufte observes that unemployment follows a four-year cycle in which the rate of unemployment is 1 to 2 percent lower on election day than it is in the previous (and future) 12 to 18 months. Hibbs and Tufte appear to be observing the same phenomena that, prior to 1972, occurred in election years when Democrats occupied the White House. It may have been Nixon's narrow 1960 defeat plus the Republican losses in the House and the Senate in 1954 and 1958, all periods of economic slowdown, which converted Nixon to Keynesian economics.[30] After 1972, there was a convergence of the two political parties on economic policy. Partisan differences become less important than the political calendar.

The existence of a four-year cycle in social welfare benefits is also supported by Kessel's content analysis of presidential statements.[31] He finds that presidents emphasize social benefits in the final year of their four-year term—as they prepare for reelection. During the second term, the evidence points to more limited influence with Congress. This pattern of presidential interest is consistent with a four-year presidential cycle in social welfare benefits.

Further evidence of the effect of the presidency on policy outcomes is found in the work of Frey and Schneider. Using a dummy variable for time before the election, they find that "presidents tend to significantly increase exhaustive government expenditures before elections."[32] This is a macroeconomic policy instrument which should theoretically result in lower unemployment. They do not, however, find this same effect with the other two macroeconomic policy instruments: government transfers and civilian jobs.

Frey and Schneider also hypothesize that the president will stimulate government expenditures in response to a decline in popularity in order to ensure reelection. This is termed the deficit popularity condition. If current popularity exceeds this critical level, termed the popularity surplus condition, the president is free to pursue his partisan or ideological goals. The coefficients of the popularity deficit are all statistically significant, indicating that expenditures are affected by their popularity levels. The coefficients of the popularity surplus variable reveal more ambiguous results. While the signs are in the expected direction for Eisenhower, Kennedy, and Nixon (although they are statistically insignificant for Eisenhower and Kennedy), the signs are negative and significant in the case of Johnson indicating that "he seems to have restricted (ceteris paribus) civilian government expenditures."[33]

The Frey and Schneider findings have not been successfully replicated by others. Increases attributed to the decreases in popularity may be a spurious effect—presidential popularity falls in response to economic downturns that result in automatic increases in government transfer payments. The ambiguous results for the surplus conditions suggest that presidential party alone does not explain patterns of government expenditures.

Other studies have further explored these relationships. Golden and Poterba examine both the effect of economic factors on presidential popularity and the relationship between the economic factors, presidential party, and electoral cycles using macroeconomic policy instruments as the dependent variable.[34] Their results indicate little evidence of any relationship between presidential popularity, electoral cycles, and macroeconomic policy. Winters and Reidenberg in an analysis of quarterly data for a number of transfer programs cast further doubt on this cyclical phenomena. They conclude "Neither the graphic evidence nor the results of multivariate analysis sustain the hypothesis of income and transfer manipulation associated with timing of the electoral cycle."[35]

These models, while important in providing some empirical form and verification to the study of the presidency and public policy, have both theoretical and measurement problems. Furthermore, these are difficulties which are shared in part by other models of the political and economic influences, which Frey terms "politico-economic models." Hibbs, Tufte, Frey and Schneider, and Golden and Poterba all start with presidentially dominated research hypotheses. All but one find support for a four-year cycle corresponding to presidential elections. Tufte argues further that there is a two-year cycle in transfer benefits which is also presidential in origin. Frey and Schneider also add popularity deficit and popularity surplus as additional presidential variables. Golden and Poterba find no evidence of electoral cycle or presidential popularity effects.

None of these models recognize other institutional factors or interactions. There is no inclusion of variables to measure partisan control of Congress and congressional committees, or the interaction between Congress and the president.[36] The models do, however, bring us to the point where we can begin to consider what alternative explanations may exist for policy influences, and serve to focus attention on the need for additional hypotheses about institutional influences and interactions between political and economic factors.

Presidential-Congressional Interaction

Partisan control of Congress may be a necessary condition for enactment of the party policy goals, but it might not be a sufficient condition. The party of the president may have at least a supporting if not confounding role. Some policy and congressional studies suggest that same party control of Congress and the presidency is a condition for policy success. Other studies suggest an opposite finding—that is, it is divided-party control of Congress which begets policy change.

A dominant thesis of many policy case studies and congressional studies is that same-party control of Congress and the presidency is a condition which enables, in the case of social welfare policy, the Democrats to enact new policies and the Republicans to curtail present programs. Ripley's typology of majorities includes three types of same-party control and one of mixed control. Under the truncated majority condition both the president and Congress are less likely to be successful in securing the enactment of policy proposals. From his analysis of five periods of tuncated majorities, Ripley concludes "to have a productive majority in the American system of government, the President and a majority of both Houses must be from the same party. Such a condition does not guarantee legislative success, but is necessary for it."[37] Similarly, Clinton Rossiter notes the necessity of this cooperation: "no great policy, domestic or foreign," he writes, "can be maintained effectively by a President without the approval of Congress in the form of laws and money."[38]

An alternative and equally plausible view emerges from other case studies but is not as widely cited in congressional analyses. These studies suggest that when Democrats control the Congress and Republicans the presidency, the Democrats will increase social spending in an effort to present themselves as the party of the people and to embarrass the president into either signing or vetoing a popular social spending program. Derthick presents evidence of a Democratic Congress outbidding the Republican president on social security benefits.[39] The bidding up of the 1972 social security increase to 20 percent is described by Tufte.[40] Manley, as well, describes the conservative posture which the Democratic Ways and Means Committee took following the election of Kennedy in 1960.[41] Fenno reports similar findings for the House Appropriations Committee.[42] Davis, Dempster, and Wildavsky find that "The Congress which was largely Democratic during the Eisenhower presidency had an extra incentive to oppose the Executive."[43] The Parker and Parker analysis of committee voting points to the importance of the partisanship of the House and the presidency as influences in voting on several committees.[44]

CHANGES IN ECONOMIC CONDITIONS

Any analysis of the relationship of politics and economics with policy outcomes must consider those economic relationships which are automatic and those in which politics and economics interact to affect the level of expenditures. Since many social welfare programs are entitlements, they expand and occasionally contract in response to fluctuations in the economy. Other adjustments to social programs are not automatic and result from decisions of legislators. These decisions are made in response to changes in economic conditions. Two relationships can be posited between economic factors and social spending; these are the effects of the level of unemployment and increases in the consumer price index.

The first explanation relates the level of unemployment to social spending. Some programs, such as unemployment compensation, are directly tied to the level of unemployment.[45] Increases in unemployment may result in the enactment of additional programs in which spending is directly related to numbers of unemployed. These include extensions of unemployment benefits and jobs programs. With other programs the relationship is indirect. For example, spending for social security and railroad retirement may increase with increased unemployment as eligible persons choose to leave the labor force by retiring. Increases in unemployment may also result in increased demand for income conditioned cash and in-kind programs such as public assistance, food stamps, and nutrition programs.

A second economic explanation concerns the relationship between price increases and the level of spending for social programs. Since inflation erodes consumer purchasing power, benefits to individuals have been periodically adjusted for inflation. Historically, social welfare benefits have been adjusted for inflation by the Congress which has responded to increases in the consumer price index (CPI). The question of how best to measure the effect of price increases and the issues of separating automatic versus legislated effects on expenditures are discussed in greater detail in chapter three.

In some models spending for social programs is not a function of political control, utility maximizing, or previous decisions, but is a function of the level of economic development. This explanation is supported by studies of social spending across nations and states. These studies have generally found that politics does not affect the level of spending for social programs.

The studies which point to economic development as the primary factor influencing social spending have been comparative in focus.[46] Jackman indicates that level of economic development is related to the degree of social equality, but that there is a threshold effect after which improvements are only marginal.[47] Cutright finds that governments which are more democratic "will tend to provide social security."[48] Jackman's findings do not support this contention. He concludes "the record does not augur well for those who would generate more social equality though more political equality."[49] In a study of social security in twenty-two countries, Aaron shows that years of experience with the program and the level of economic development are the most important variables in explaining program expenditure levels.[50] Wilensky finds that economic development mediated by age of population and age of the program is the major influence on social spending in sixty-four countries.[51] In a longitudinal study of social spending in Sweden, Peters demonstrates phases to the pattern of expenditures.[52] Political mobilization is an early influence, increasingly bureaucracies become more influential, and finally economic development is a key factor. In a summary of the findings of the comparative policy studies of income maintenance programs, Heidenheimer, Heclo, and Adams conclude:

> It is significant that one can discuss the growth of programs, coverage, and standards without necessarily referring to the differences between political systems. . . . Nor does spending on these programs appear to differ significantly because of differing political arrangements. . . . the research has generally shown that, for a very broad range of countries, economic development rather than political make-up is associated with the level of welfare effort (assuming that by effort we mean a ratio of social insurance spending to national income).[53]

This research should not lead us to modify too quickly expectations about the influence of politics on U.S. social welfare policies. First, the measures used in these studies are rather broad. The most common one is spending as a percent of national product. These measures are useful when comparing expenditures across nations but can obscure variation in policies in a single nation. When one considers the number and vast array of social programs in any country, each of which may be affected differently by economics and demographics at a given point, it is not surprising that variations in economic and demographic variables are more closely related to the policy variable than is variation in the more stable political variables.[54]

A second observation about these economic studies is that many are cross-sectional. Longitudinal studies have shown that there are phases in social spending across time. A measure of all expenditures at a single point can obscure patterns observed in separate programs across time. In this study we will be using measures of total spending, measures of single programs, and analyzing programs longitudinally. This approach may indicate relationships not observed in cross-sectional comparative studies. The relationship between levels of economic growth and social welfare benefits can be more precisely specified by using economic time series such as wages, prices, and disposable income. These relationships are important because benefits are designed to provide a level of income support to individuals. The government devotes considerable effort to estimate the relationships which these programs have to economic conditions. Political factors are rarely included in these models and legislative increases are considered exogenous. Yet we know that policy makers are keenly aware of economic conditions when deciding to modify benefits. These economic and political relationships must be considered as policy predictors.

Two aspects of these relationships between economic conditions and policy outcomes can be examined. One is the extent to which the effect of economic conditions on benefits varies across programs. This is a substantively interesting relationship which can help us to understand whether some types of individuals, different program recipients, fare better than others. Second, we are interested in the existence of interactions between partisan and economic factors. Have benefits kept pace with inflation or gains in real wages during Democratic administrations as well as during Republican administrations? What effect, if any, have the other institutional factors had under certain economic conditions?

29

CYCLICAL REGULARITIES IN THE POLITICAL CALENDAR

A number of recent studies have suggested that there may be a cyclical explanation for patterns of growth in government spending. In the political business cycle explanations, politicians cater to the public's short-sighted vision and seek to reduce unemployment near election day at the cost of increased inflation.[55] Tufte describes a two-year electoral cycle in personal income and transfer benefits (primarily OASDI and veterans' benefits) and a four-year cycle in unemployment. Manipulation in unemployment, Tufte argues, requires more "macroeconomic skill."[56] In Frey and Schneider's time series estimation, they find that total government expenditures increase before elections but not transfer payments or numbers of government civilian employees.[57] Golden and Poterba find no evidence of cyclical patterns with macroeconomic instruments, including transfers.[58] They do concede, consistent with Tufte's argument, however, that politicians may try to manipulate the economy. Evidence of success, they argue, is lacking.

One difficulty with the electoral cycle explanations is that they contain implicit assumptions about institutional and political influences and ignore other equally plausible influences. For instance, Frey and Schneider and Tufte each describe a presidential dominated cycle. The congressional influence in the electoral cycle is not explored in any of the models cited above. Tufte does concede that the 20 percent social security increase in 1972 resulted from the bidding up of the Republican president's request by a Democratic Congress. However, in referring to the flow of transfer payments to individuals, for which Tufte coins the term "kyphosis," meaning that agencies accelerate processing of applications and payments prior to elections, he attributes this increase to a bureaucracy responsive to the president. "Kyphosis is a sign of presidential power."[59] This reasoning ignores both the mutual or independent interest of Congress in reelection and its influence on policy and the bureaucracy.

The social security increases enacted during the Eisenhower years were passed over presidential opposition.[60] It may be that a condition for benefit increases is a Democratic Congress and a Republican president. Recent congressional literature has demonstrated congressional interest in casework, and social security is a case where work is often needed.[61] The close working relationship between Congress and the bureaucracy is described in many studies of subgovernments, committees, and policy.[62] A variety of explanations concerning the electoral cycle or other political cycles could be posited. These might include a four-year cycle, a two-year cycle, the interaction of control of the presidency, the Congress, and the occurrence of elections, and finally a "presidential honeymoon cycle." The latter, suggested by many case studies, would indicate that presidents might be more successful in programmatic initiatives in the first year of their administrations.[63]

PREVIOUS DECISIONS OF POLITICAL ACTORS

A final explanation of policy making found in the literature is incrementalism. This explanation is consistent with the dynamics of the congressional policy process. That process is characterized by stability of membership and by committees chaired by members whose tenure spans presidential administrations. Fenno and Wildavsky have analyzed this process in terms of decision making and the range of decisions of that process rather than from the standpoint of policy outcomes.[64] Although a common approach of many studies is to note exceptions to the incremental decision rule and to specify when and with what types of policy nonincremental changes occur, there has been little attention given to how changes in Congress may be responsible for departures from the incremental decision rule.

Since many social welfare programs are entitlements which pay benefits to all eligible individuals, previous policy decisions are a major factor determining current expenditures. These entitlements are a major component of the 75 percent of the U.S. budget termed "uncontrollable." The issue of measuring the effect of previous decisions on current expenditures is discussed in more detail in the following chapter. In subsequent chapters, the lags between policy decisions and policy outcomes are examined. Also considered is the extent to which the increased expenditures observed during the Nixon and Ford presidencies were the result of policy initiatives enacted during their presidencies or whether they result from decisions made during the Johnson years.

COMMITTEE JURISDICTION AND POLICY DIVERSITY

The effect of committee differences on policy in any comparative sense has been largely neglected. We know much about the role of individual committees at particular points. Studies of the Appropriations Committees and the Ways and Means Committee do discuss social security issues.[65] Similarly, case studies of particular policies also describe the committees' pivotal role in shaping policy. See, for example, Derthick on social security or Moynihan and Bowler on welfare reform.[66] The set of studies that look at policy effects across committees, across policies, or across time is very small indeed.[67]

The dominant thesis of this literature is twofold. First, it is asserted, without much qualification, that committees affect policy. The conditions of this influence are less clearly understood. It is important to analyze committee influence with respect to the other institutional and policy effects which also affect policy. These are what Fenno terms external constraints.[68] The second thesis of the committee literature is that committees differ. The implication of this literature is that these committee differences may result in differences in the manner and extent to which committees affect policy. These are the strategic premises of committees.[69] The policy implications of these committee differences also need to be more systematically examined.

The majority of the policies analyzed here fall within the jurisdiction of five committees in the House and five in the Senate. The House committees are Ways and Means; Agriculture; Banking and Currency; Education and Labor; and Veterans. These committees have jurisdiction over the major social programs. About five additional committees in each body have jurisdiction over a small number of policies.

Each of these committees differs in its environmental constraints, member goals, and strategic premises. The Ways and Means Committee was long considered the most prestigious House Committee which dealt with some of the most controversial and important legislation: taxes and social security. Both Fenno and Manley suggest that the Ways and Means Committee influences the legislation in a way that is noncontroversial and acceptable to the House.[71] Referring to social security, Fenno observes, "Incremental adjustments in the core program, however, have become accepted national policy, commanding a bipartisan consensus."[72] It is a reasonable inference from the committee literature that a conflictual partisan committee such as the House Education and Labor Committee would not have produced a consensual, accepted policy such as the social security program. Yet, the extent to which policies vary because of their differing committee jurisdictions has not been very thoroughly examined.

Other committees differ in characteristics which might be expected to have policy consequences. The Agriculture Committee has long been dominated by farm state representatives and has developed a strategic premise in which subcommittee decisions are accepted by the full committee and the committee decisions are accepted by the House. If, as some have argued, process affects policy, then the food stamp program might be processed not much differently than potato subsidies.[73] Thus, food stamps to the Agriculture Committee would appear more like an agriculture policy than an incomes policy. A similar program enacted by the Ways and Means Committee would have different policy characteristics and would be affected by the processes of that committee.

If the reverse were true, however, that the policy affects the process then the subject matter and purposes of the food stamp program would evoke a different set of policy interests. Thus, the food stamp program consideration on the House floor would differ from the consideration of other agriculture matters. The committee's policy recommendation might be amended on the House floor.

These are important questions about the nature of the policy process in Congress. They can be posed similarly for housing and veterans' programs, income maintenance programs under the jurisdiction of the Banking and Currency Committee and Veterans' Affairs Committee.

Another unexplained committee factor is the influence of environmental constraints on policy outcomes as mitigated through committees. Three environmental influences are the partisan composition of the House and the Senate, the party of the president, and influences originating from the policy itself. These constraints can be viewed as external factors operating on committees. These factors might be expected to influence policy outcomes and may vary with committee. Referring to the first of these environmental influences, Fenno indicates: "Committee partisanship is not constant across periods of time, but is sensitive to changing external partisan alignments, i.e. to changes in party control of the presidency and party strength in the House. If we are correct—such changes should, in turn, affect the content of committee decisions."[74] Fenno does present evidence of the influence of a Democratic president on the volume of committee decisions of the Education and Labor Committee. Unanswered, however, is how this influence of the Democratic president varies when we consider not Education and Labor but the Ways and Means Committee with its norm of restrained partisanship. Thus, the partisan composition of Congress may have a policy effect which varies with committees.

Pressures originating from the policy itself or from economic factors which have an impact on the policy may also be considered environmental constraints. "Partisanship on social security matters occurs only when major policy departures (those of 1962 and 1965 for example) are at stake," Fenno writes.[75] This discussion suggests that some committees, Ways and Means in this instance, may be more insulated from partisan changes but are still sensitive to economic or policy influences which require policy modification and may evoke partisanship. Manley has noted that "political scientists have not given sufficient emphasis to substantive consideration of policy questions as a variable that helps explain the actions of policy makers."[76] Committees are an important stage in the congressional policy process where substantive policy considerations should affect policy outcomes.

In the absence of environmental constraints such as political or policy pressures, one might expect committees to have a dampening effect on policy change. The acceptance of committee expertise, their procedural jurisdiction in the legislative process, and the stability of committee membership should all act to support the continuation of the status quo.[77]

Summarizing this discussion, we can enumerate several aspects of committees which previous studies have suggested will have policy effects. First, committee differences themselves should affect policy outcomes. This means that policies may vary because jurisdiction is with different committees. Second, stability in committee membership should support stability and continuity in policy. Changes in committee membership will provide conditions for policy change. Third, the influence of environmental constraints, partisan composition of the Congress, the party of the president, and pressures from policy or economic influences will vary with committees. In subsequent chapters, we do not explicitly use a committee variable in the analysis, but since the social welfare programs do have different committee jurisdictions, some differences due to committees can be observed.

CONCLUSION

In this chapter we have set forth five explanations of influences on policy which have been drawn from the empirical literature on Congress and the presidency and from analyses of particular social welfare policies. These were described as 1) decisions of political actors; 2) economic effects; 3) political calendar effects; 4) previous decisions; and 5) committee jurisdiction. The political actors we consider are the Congress and the presidency. The size of the majority party in Congress, the party of the president, and the leadership and partisan composition of particular congressional committee with jurisdiction over the social welfare program are expected to affect policy decisions for the 170 federal social welfare programs. Issues of measuring social policy and assessing the effect of these political and economic indicators on those policy measures are discussed in more detail in the following chapter. In chapter four, the characteristics of specific social programs are outlined. Throughout the balance of the book the effect of the political and economic influences described here are shown to affect these measures of social programs.

3

Measuring Social
Welfare Policy

Linking the political and economic influences described in chapter two with indicators of United States social welfare policy, requires the consideration of a number of conceptual and measurement issues. The conceptual issues include distinguishing between policy influences, policy decisions, policy outcomes, and policy impacts and specifying interrelationships between these concepts. The measurement issues, which arise from the definitions of these concepts, include problems in analyzing entitlement and other uncontrollable expenditures; measuring past decisions which affect current expenditures; and assessing economic effects on expenditures.

CONCEPTUAL ISSUES AND DEFINITIONS

Various terms have been used to describe policy variables. Some have used measures they call outputs; others describe policy outcomes; still others have analyzed policy impacts. Any distinctions which may have once existed among these terms have been blurred by the varied usage which has followed their original, less than precise, definitions.[1] In this analysis we will use and define the following terms to clarify the numerous concepts underlying a limited set of measures.

Policy influences. These are political, economic, and demographic factors which affect policy decisions, outcomes, and impacts. For this analysis the political factors are the party control of the presidency and the Congress.

Policy decisions. A policy decision is a change in a social welfare program as a result of actions by the executive or the legislature. For this study we define these actions as presidential policy or budget recommendations made in executive documents, speeches, or committee testimony. Legislative decisions are actions taken in committees, floor votes, and final actions of the Congress. For social welfare policy, a decision is an action to increase or decrease expenditures or benefits, to tighten or loosen program eligibility, or to otherwise modify conditions of assistance.

Policy outcomes. Policy outcomes are defined as the results of policy decisions. They are the actual consequences of the decisions. In the social welfare context, outcomes are program expenditures or average benefits paid to individuals. Given the uncertainties of human behavior and of policy forecasting and implementation, outcomes are not always predictable from decisions.

Policy impacts. Policy impacts are the effects of the policy outcomes measured on an individual or an aggregate basis. To continue the social welfare example, an impact is an increase in personal income, or a decrease in the number of persons with incomes less than the poverty line. Impacts are measured achievements of policy goals.

These definitions and their underlying concepts are linked through the relationships indicated in Figure 3-1.[2] The focus of this analysis is decidedly limited to U.S. federal social welfare and to just part of the process outlined in Figure 3-1. Hence, the policy influences and perhaps the measurement problems will differ from those observed for other policy areas. There are, how-

FIGURE 3-1
Policy Indicators for Social Welfare

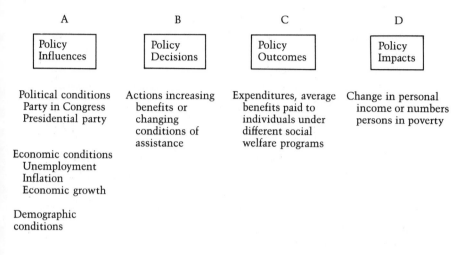

A	B	C	D
Policy Influences	Policy Decisions	Policy Outcomes	Policy Impacts
Political conditions Party in Congress Presidential party	Actions increasing benefits or changing conditions of assistance	Expenditures, average benefits paid to individuals under different social welfare programs	Change in personal income or numbers persons in poverty
Economic conditions Unemployment Inflation Economic growth			
Demographic conditions			

ever, commonalities shared with all policy analyses which the scheme in Figure 3-1 and the definitions address.

The primary focus of this analysis is the linkage of political influences to policy decisions made by political actors and to the policy outcomes which result from the decisions. The policy influences are those which are known to be important in Congress and which are thought to have policy effects. They include the party of the president, the number of nonsouthern Democrats elected to Congress, the occurrence of elections, and whether it is early or late in the presidential administration. Economic conditions, such as levels of unemployment, prices, and per capita income have also been used as predictors of policy change. Demographic variables, measured as number of persons over sixty-five or less than eighteen, are another set of policy influences. There are certainly parallels between these influences and those found in the comparative state policy literature. Many analyses have linked policy influences directly with some measure of outcomes or impacts (Path A $->$ C). The "uncontrollable" nature of expenditures for U.S. social welfare programs presents problems for models which we term determinant-outcome linkage models.[3] Since many social programs are entitlements, changes in benefits or increases in expenditures are not necessarily the result of decisions made in the current or even the previous fiscal year. The relationships between influences and outcomes in the current fiscal year may be spurious because the true relationship involves some unspecified lag period. The problem appears even more intractable when one considers the variety of U.S. social programs, each with a potentially different lag relationship. The definitions and specification of the concepts in Figure 3-1 allow us to address this problem.

Policy decisions are an intermediate variable which measure whether there was any action to increase or decrease benefits or to otherwise affect the level of expenditures. They are a link between policy influences and policy outcomes. Decisions to increase benefits made by the executive or the legislature result from changes in political factors interacting with economic conditions. Decisions are more proximate to policy influences than are outcomes. Decisions, however, are policy specific as well as specific to the actions of the president, the House, and the Senate.

Outcomes result from policy decisions. In a given year these outcomes are the total expenditures or average program benefits of social programs. Both total expenditures and average program benefits are summary measures of individual benefit formula, numbers of eligible beneficiaries, economic conditions, demographic factors, and political decisions. For social programs, actual expenditures are more appropriate outcome measures than are authorization and appropriation levels. For housing and education programs, appropriation levels were consistently below authorizations. For payments to individuals, appropriation levels are often only estimates based on best guesses of the numbers of beneficiaries and economic conditions. Before the mid

1960s expenditures for the trust funds—social security, Civil Service Retirement, and unemployment compensation—were not included in the Labor-HEW appropriation bill as they are today. While reflective of congressional decisions, authorization and appropriations levels are not solely the outcomes of congressional actions.

The last linkage in the policy relationship in Figure 3-1 is to policy impacts, which are defined here as the end results of policy outcomes. The impacts are indicators of the goals of public programs. The percentage of persons at less than poverty level, indicators of educational attainment, and measures of malnutrition are examples of policy impacts. The analysis of the success of program expenditures in achieving program goals we associate with policy evaluation. It is the aspect of this analysis to which we will devote the least attention. The purpose in describing this linkage is to make clear the distinctions in measuring policy which have oftentimes been blurred and to demonstrate that, with careful conceptualization and measurement, the impact of political control can ultimately be traced to its impact on measures of economic well-being.

The formulation of a complete model of the policy process is certainly much more complex than this brief schema depicts. The primary emphasis here is to separate the effect of political and economic influences acting through policy decisions from those automatic effects which influence outcomes directly. Policy decisions might increase benefits while at the same time changing economic conditions could result in an overall decrease in total expenditures. Social expenditures, which are largely entitlements, require this decomposition in order to show political and economic effects.

MEASUREMENT ISSUES

Several measurement issues underlie the conceptualization outlined here. These include the measurement of entitlement programs, the assessment of the effect of previous decisions, and the analysis of the impact of economic changes on program benefits. Each of these are issues which confront any analysis of U.S. social programs.

The Entitlement Problem

The growth of federal social programs requires a reconsideration of some commonly used measures of policy: congressional appropriations. Studies such as Fenno's analysis of the appropriations process have relied on the comparison of agency requests, presidential recommendations, committee decisions, and floor votes to analyze policy choices.[4] Fenno's appropriations categories bear little relationship to current budget categories and decisions. His analysis and the many which extended it were organized around expenditures for agencies and predictable government programs. Analyses which followed Fenno's have found that program expenditures may invoke different decision rules than agency expenditures.[5]

The nature and size of federal expenditures from 1947 to 1962, the period of Fenno's analysis, have changed dramatically. Today 75 percent of the federal budget is termed "relatively uncontrollable." Sum-sufficient appropriations, multiyear appropriations, trust fund expenditures, and entitlement programs, which in the past were referred to as backdoor spending, overshadow the agency and program expenditures of the type which Fenno analyzed. Today only 15 percent of the budget is designated for agencies and discretionary grants.[6] There are about sixty programs that can be termed entitlements constituting over 50 percent of the federal budget.[7] Most would agree that budget decisions for the Social Security Administration, one of Fenno's agencies, would differ considerably from budget decisions for social security program benefits, an entitlement program. During the period of Fenno's analysis, few entitlement programs beyond the retirement programs existed.

Despite this change in the character of federal expenditures, Fenno's study serves as an excellent example of a very careful effort to address the same questions we are raising here about how to assess institutional effects on policy. The introductory remarks in *The Power of the Purse* remain a succinct statement of this problem.[8]

> Whether one wishes to generalize about the outcome of the appropriations sequence or whether one wishes to generalize about the output of a committee as a system, one must know what kinds of decisions get made. Decisions, that is, are a critical dependent variable in process-oriented research. Too often in legislative research, we describe the process of decision-making in great detail yet cannot relate process to outcome—because we simply cannot describe the decisions that result. It is enormously helpful, in this case, to be able to characterize appropriations decisions and base generalizations about them on quantified evidence.

It is necessary, however, to devise new measures of decisions to accommodate changes in federal programs and policy making. The change in federal expenditures has two implications for this research. First, for some programs appropriation figures have little bearing on actual expenditures. Hence their usefulness as policy outcomes is limited. Expenditures are determined by exogenous factors interacting with legislatively enacted formula. Congress routinely relies on supplemental appropriations when expenditures exceed appropriated amounts. Second, for entitlement programs, appropriation levels are limited as indicators of executive and legislative policy decisions. In the decision process political actors often tinker with the formula and eligibility criteria when making decisions on entitlement programs without fully understanding the effects of these changes. Appropriations targets were available, but they often had less salience than did estimates of average benefits or numbers of affected beneficiaries.

Congress has on occasion sought to cap program expenditures as a way to hold down expenditures. This was a successful method to halt the growth of social service grants to states which were growing to keep up with the requirement that the federal government match 75 percent of state expenditures.[9] This type of cap has not worked with programs which pay benefits to individuals because the government ultimately pays when additional beneficiaries qualify after the cap has been reached. The Ways and Means Committee imposed a cap on AFDC expenditures in 1967 which President Nixon refused to implement. Congress has increased appropriations for food stamps several times when the appropriation level was reached. The Reconciliation Act of 1981 did contain caps for several social programs.

The issue of entitlements should not be construed to suggest that political factors do not matter and that expenditures are determined only by economic conditions and other exogenous factors. Rather, it requires that we consider a different calculus of budgeting with policy measures appropriate for analyzing entitlement decisions. It is important to remember that all entitlement programs are created by acts of Congress.

The fiscal 1971 budget first introduced the concept of uncontrollability. The first use of the term recognized its ambiguity. As the budget document states, "In addition to these cases, the concept of 'controllability' embraces areas where distinctions are blurred. Therefore, it is more accurate to refer to outlays as being 'relatively' controllable or uncontrollable."[10]

The real issues of controllability are the sensitivity of expenditures to economic conditions, the accuracy of the estimates of program participation, and the willingness of Congress and the president to consider program modifications. President Reagan sought to reduce the sensitivity through delays and modifications of the cost of living provisions. The elasticity of expenditures to economic conditions is in part discretionary. In response to increasing unemployment, extended unemployment programs are enacted and supplemental appropriations are granted for programs such as food stamps. The fiscal 1985 budget notes that "In recent years, legislative changes, administrative reforms, and economic developments have reduced the acute sensitivity of the budget to economic assumptions."[11]

Thus, the term "uncontrollable" is actually a misnomer. All expenditures are ultimately controllable if Congress wishes to change the authorizing law or to impose or enforce caps on de facto entitlement programs. The Reconciliation Act of 1981 serves as a very recent and potent reminder of this fact. In that act the Congress made 200 program changes designed to reduce expenditures over $100 billion in fiscal 1982, 1983, and 1984.[12] To analyze these social programs we need to reevaluate the utility of authorization and appropriation levels and consider other measures of policy decisions.

The difference between congressional and presidential budgeting is also a problem for analysis of social programs. Presidents estimate expenditures for entitlements based upon estimated numbers of eligible beneficiaries and benefit levels. Congress usually accepts these estimates unless it has updated economic or program data which project demand to be greater than forecast in the president's budget.

Measuring the Effects of Previous Decisions

The second measurement issue is the existence of lags between policy decisions and policy outcomes and the problem of assessing the effect of previous policy decisions. It also illustrates problems with commonly used measures. This problem occurs with determinant-outcome linkage models and is manifest in two ways. The first case concerns the observation of an effect between a policy determinant and a policy outcome, but where the effect is spurious. The real cause is some unobserved variable. If the increase in expenditures is the result of some previous policy decision, then the political determinant that is affecting expenditures is one which occurred in a previous time period. The second manifestation of this problem is the obverse situation. In a particular time period, we may observe some

45

political or economic changes, but no change in policy outcomes. The effect of a policy decision made today might not be observed until a future time period. Determinant-outcome linkage models are particularly prone to this type of specification error.

The problem of assessing the effect of previous policy decisions is also seen in the debates over incrementalism. The concept of incrementalism has gained ready acceptance because of its intuitive appeal and its confirmation by everyday experience, but it has analytical shortcomings.[13] For some, incrementalism has been a descriptive and at times a normative concept. Among others, it has promoted a tangential discussion of the measurement and definition of an increment. Much of this discussion has missed the distinction between outcomes and decisions. An incremental decision process could very easily give rise to nonincremental outcomes. For example, to extend program eligibility to widows and orphans is a logical, incremental modification of social policy. Yet the resulting programmatic expenditures may show a dramatic increase. Any analysis of expenditures without proper attention to the measurement of decisions and outcomes would misdescribe this policy process.

The ambiguity of the concept is particularly apparent in social welfare policy. One characteristic of social welfare expenditures in recent years has been the unexpected, explosive growth in certain programs. Did policy makers and congresspersons think they were making nonincremental decisions in enacting the Medicaid program? Most analysts would say no, but the outcomes show rapid growth. Similarly, Albritton describes SSI as nonincremental based on changes in outcomes, but Bowler, emphasizing the conceptual process rather than the outcomes, characterizes the decision as much more incremental.[14] To Steiner, the series of decisions which has resulted in the myriad programs of U.S. social welfare policy represent "tireless tinkering."[15] In a similar fashion, Moynihan describes the Nixon family assistance program as a nonincremental proposal for a policy marked by incremental changes.[16]

The cumulative effect of small adjustments may lead to large scale reform as unintended consequences create pressures for change, observe Heidenheimer, Heclo, and Adams. They state

> Once an important boundary is crossed and the dust of political controversy has settled somewhat, all sides of the political spectrum tend to accept the inherited structure of income maintenance policy and to busy themselves with what are regarded as incremental improvements in existing policy. But because this step-by-step approach can produce a cumulative outcome that no one intended, a subtle potential exists for radical change within incrementalism. Once the cumulative impact of many small changes is felt and questioned, the state may be set for a new period of more fundamental debate about boundary issues and policy realignment.[17]

These different interpretations illustrate the importance of being cognizant of the concepts about the policy process underlying policy measurement.

Several remedies to this problem of assessing previous policy effects are possible. One is to decide upon appropriate lag relationships between the political and economic variables and the policy outcomes. These lags are derived from a substantive understanding of the particular programs. Specifying appropriate lags for political and economic effects is always somewhat arbitrary. When too many different programs are aggregated the assumptions about lag effects can be much too tenuous.

A second remedy is to control for the effect of previous expenditures so that all other contemporaneous variables explain only that portion of the variance not explained by previous expenditures. This can be done by using the previous level of expenditures as a predictor variable. This alternative does not directly measure the lag between political changes and policy effect but does bring previous decisions directly into the model. It is a way of operationalizing the concept of incrementalism. What we spend today is in large part determined by what we spent before plus the effect of contemporaneous factors.

Variants on this remedy are utilized in several studies and demonstrate the transition of incrementalism from a descriptive concept to an analytical concept through the use of time series regression.[18] Davis, Dempster, and Wildavsky, in their early models predicted current appropriations from previous appropriations and current requests. There remained, however, exceptions and breaks in the series which the models did not predict. Subsequent extended models included "political, economic and social exogenous variables."[19] Wanat has decomposed appropriations into their base, the mandatory request, and the programmatic request in an analysis of 68 line items in five Labor appropriations bills from fiscal year 1968 to fiscal year 1972. He finds "that the base was practically untouched by Congress, while the increment was cut by more than 5 percent."[20] In another time series of social expenditures in seven democracies, Bunce finds that " 'The routines of politics,' to borrow Sharkansky's phrase, are disturbed by elections and changes in administrations."[21]

A related approach is the current services concept adopted by the Senate Budget Committee and now by OMB. The budget documents define current service estimates as a:

> . . . base (which) embodies the cumulative effect of all past congressional and presidential budgetary choices. . . . For entitlement programs (such as social security) the current services estimates take into account inflation adjustments that are mandatory under current law, changes in the benefit base (usually determined by past earnings), and changes in the anticipated number of beneficiaries.[22]

These measures are available only from the mid-seventies on. They embody a good number of economic and behavioral assumptions and have been used as a budget strategy.[23] As a base for evaluating current budget recommendations and choices the measures have much to commend them.

The third remedy is to use an intermediate set of variables—a variable between influences and outcomes—which reflects policy decisions. With large programs which are elastic relative to formula changes, the intermediate variable can be used simply to confirm that changes in outcomes are responsive to policy decisions. For example, an examination of the average benefit series for retired persons under social security shows that changes in the benefit formula are reflected as changes in this series. A formula change designed to increase benefits 7 percent is reflected in a 7.7 percent change in benefits in the month the benefit change was to take effect. This relationship is closer than that of other series because the social security personnel were skilled and familiar with the manipulations to the benefit formula.[24]

In a well-behaved series such as social security, the effect of predicting outcomes from policy influences would be much the same as predicting policy decisions. One series is a reflection of the other. All benefit series are not so inclined to predictable patterns. Programs such as Medicare and Medicaid are much less manipulatable and less able to be forecast than are other programs. For these programs, decision measures can be used as intermediate variables to analyze the effect of policy influences. Expenditures for some social programs have tended to grow much more rapidly with fewer policy decisions than other federal programs.[25]

To analyze the effect of previous expenditures we use two approaches. The first is to use intermediate indicators of decisions. These include indicators of presidential and congressional policy initiation, recommendations to modify or adjust benefits, and presidential budget and legislative recommendations. These indicators permit the pinpointing of when decisions were made which are expected to affect policy outcomes. The second method is to analyze percentage changes in expenditures. This calculation permits us to focus on those changes at the margin. Changes are measured relative to the base in units which are comparable across the years even as the size of expenditures dramatically increases.

Measuring the Effect of Price Changes

The final problem which occurs in these analyses is the issue of how to analyze the effect of price changes. Economists argue that the only way policy series should be examined are in real terms, that is, adjusted to remove inflation effects. In order to compare benefits received during different time periods, it is necessary, the argument goes, to examine the purchasing power of benefits in common, deflated dollars. While this argument makes sense for many analyses, some information is lost through this approach.

In social welfare benefit series, price increases can be seen as a cause which often interacts with political conditions to result in benefit increases. For some analyses, it is useful to assess whether recipients receive a real benefit increase or simply keep up with inflation. An alternative approach is to examine when inflation adjustments are made and whether they are triggered by price changes alone or price changes interacting with conditions of political control. This approach requires a measure of policy decisions.

Changes in the consumer price index provide a base for calculating benefit increases, but it has been political factors which have determined when these social security increases were enacted. One of these political factors was the cost of living adjustments recommended by presidents in their first terms. These recommendations were always equal to the price increases since the last benefit increase, but there was no effort to raise the absolute level of social security benefits by presidents in their first year in office. These recommendations, however, provided legislators an opportunity to increase benefits further. Interest in these increases was especially keen in election years. Inflation serves as the base; political events determine the size and the timing of the increases.

For years Congress adjusted transfer benefits for price increases on an *ad hoc* basis, but today most benefit programs are indexed for inflation. Two programs, Civil Service Retirement and Military Retirement, were indexed effective in 1965 and 1964, respectively. The major push for indexation occurred from 1971 to 1975 when social security (1975), food stamps (1971), Railroad Retirement (1975), Supplemental Security Income (1975), and child nutrition programs (1971–75) were indexed.[26] The differences between *ad hoc* and indexed benefit increases as well as the developments which led to indexing are discussed in chapter seven.

The implication of this discussion is that it is necessary to separate price increases as a policy determinant and to analyze the interaction of prices with political factors. Analyzing real benefit levels is useful in making comparisons across programs and to analyze expenditures in the latter part of the series when programs are indexed. Throughout the book the expenditures are presented in real terms in most of the tables. In order to analyze the political and economic conditions which led to benefit adjustments, in chapter seven we rely on indicators of presidential and congressional decisions to assess how benefits have kept pace with price changes. For that analysis, the goal is to understand the process by which price changes interact with political control and trigger changes in federal program benefits.

TOWARD NEW MEASURES OF SOCIAL WELFARE POLICY

Thus far we have suggested that the analysis of political influences on policy has been hampered by the lack of policy measures which are comparable across programs and which can be linked to political institutions. This problem can be termed as one of too many concepts chasing too few measures. If the concepts can be disentangled as we propose through the definitions and through the measurement and analytical approaches outlined here, a key question remains. Are there measures which permit analysis of these concepts separately?

For this discussion we will leave aside consideration of the measurement of policy influences and policy impacts. There is less argument about the former, and we subscribe to the position that if the questions about measuring policy can be resolved, many measures and explanations of political influences are available for testing. On the issue of policy impacts, some caution should be exercised in linking policy influences with policy impacts directly. While it is interesting to ask whether the number of persons at less than the poverty level has increased during Republican administrations or decreased during periods of Democratic congressional control, any analysis of this sort must be explicitly aware of the causal linkage between the influences and the policy impact. If we choose not to analyze the intermediate steps, we are vulnerable to the risks of spurious correlations. While these linkages have been successfully modeled by some, the approach we propose makes this linkage more explicit through the policy measurement and analysis.

Policy outcomes have been defined herein as results of policy decisions. Outcomes are measured as levels of program expenditures or average benefits. These are the dollars actually spent or the benefits actually received in a given year. Average benefits provide a more direct individual level measure. They are calculated by dividing total program benefits by the number of recipients. This measure has several desirable characteristics. It is a visible measure which policy makers are aware of as they make adjustments to benefit formula. Thus it has the necessary linkage to the decision process. Finally, it is a measure which is comparable across programs and does not include administrative expenses.

Program expenditures are also comparable across programs, but they are not the visible program indicators which average benefits are. Policy makers and legislators are not always fully aware of the effect that program adjustments will have on program expenditures. This measure is, however, a useful summary indicator for those programs where an average benefit is not available or meaningful. Manpower and employment programs or child nutrition programs are examples.

The measures of policy outcomes used in previous time series have been broader indicators of social policy. The political business cycle literature focuses on trade-offs between levels of inflation and unemployment.[27] Hibbs and Tufte have analyzed the existence of cycles of political influence on levels of unemployment and inflation.[28] The analysis of economic effects has been extended to macroeconomic instruments which affect the level of unemployment and inflation. The political economic models have used indicators of government economic activity. These include total expenditures, transfers, government jobs, money supply, deficits, and surpluses.[29] Golden and Poterba standardize these measures as percents of full employment GNP. Others who are interested in comparing sizes of public economic activity have used various measures of spending as percents of GNP or per capita gross domestic product. These comparisons are usually cross-national.

Several studies of U.S. expenditures have used budget data. These include the Davis, Dempster, and Wildavsky predictive model of expenditures. Bozeman analyzes expenditures for separate agency budgets.[30] Caldeira and Cowart analyze expenditures for criminal justice programs.[31] These studies, and particularly those of single agencies, have a close relationship with budgeting studies that have always used appropriations and expenditure data.

These policy measures, with the exception of the budget data, are not linked directly to political decisions. Both average benefits and program expenditures are summary measures of a variety of decisions which affect social welfare expenditures. These include adjustments of benefit formula, changes in eligibility requirements or conditions of assistance, increases in program funding, or changes in federal contributions. These decisions, coupled with economic conditions and individual behavior, determine the level of program expenditures.

This approach represents an effort to develop measures of social welfare policy which can, in Fenno's words, "relate process to outcomes." Social welfare policy with their uncontrollable expenditures, lagged decision effects, and their relationships with prices cause particular problems for analyses relating political influences and policy. To analyze these relationships we must be aware of the concepts underlying the measures. Measures of outcomes, such as average benefits and program expenditures, are available for social welfare policy. It is for policy decisions, the link which relates influences to outcomes, that we have too few measures. The analysis of the relationship of politics with policy requires that we consider carefully the concepts underlying the measures. In chapters five through seven we will utilize measures of decisions, outcomes, and impacts developed along the lines indicated in this chapter. First, however, we discuss specific United States social welfare programs and their classification.

4

Policies, Programs, and Expenditures

United States social welfare programs are categorical and fragmented. Furthermore, these programs fall within the jurisdiction of about a dozen congressional committees. To understand how decisions on social programs have been made, we need to look in detail at the components which comprise the multiple aspects of U.S. social policy and to examine the alternative ways these programs are classified. From this discussion, the character and conditions of U.S. social programs become more apparent.

SOCIAL WELFARE PROGRAMS

The basic unit of this analysis is a social welfare program. This emphasis is an important departure from many previous studies of the budget process. Fenno's analysis and those which followed have an agency focus.[1] Now with only about 15 percent of the federal budget allotted to the programs which Fenno studied, analyses of this type focus on decisions which are described as routine. The main concerns of politicians and policy makers today are with the uncontrollable aspects of the budget—particularly the social programs which we analyze. Sharkansky has found that budgeting for programs at the state level did not show the same patterns of regularity that agency budgets evidenced.[2] Analyzing program decisions requires much more effort to collect data and requires the untangling of jurisdictional issues and political decisions which lead to subsequent program growth.[3]

There is no agreement as to what constitutes a program. There are at least three possible definitions that could be used. One is the program classification of the federal budget; the second is the *Catalog of Federal Domestic Assistance* (CFDA) listing; and the third is the Social Security Administration series program definitions.

Budget Accounts

Some analysts have used budget accounts in the executive budget as the basis for programs; for example, a recent report of the Congressional Research Service identified twenty-seven "major human resource programs."[4] The criteria for inclusion were that they exist within four budget categories and have 1982 budget authority or outlays of $1 billion or more. These twenty-seven programs comprise 90 percent of all federal human resource expenditures. The definition of a program in this series is determined by federal budget accounts between 1970 and 1984. By this rule, one program is Child Nutrition. By another rule, however, these Child Nutrition programs would be considered as about eight programs. In addition, there are other programs under the Women, Infant, and Children (WIC) and Special Milk budget accounts which are not included because they are separate budget accounts which are less than $1 billion. These program budget accounts do have the desirable characteristic of being accounts for which Congress appropriates money specifically. Program budget accounts, however, are not fixed for very long stretches; they are revised as programs grow and are reorganized.

Federal Domestic Assistance Classification

An alternative program definition is the one found in the federal publication *Catalog of Federal Domestic Assistance (CFDA)*. The *CFDA* enumerates over 1000 federal programs authorized under federal laws. A program in this catalog might be "called a program, an activity, a service, a project, a process, or some other name, regardless of whether it is identified as a separate program by statute or regulation."[5] Generally, this designation is used to distinguish programs which are targeted to different groups or have different eligibility conditions. The Child Nutrition Program budget category contains six *CFDA* programs. Another eight food programs are contained in other budget categories. These programs are usually designated as activities within the federal budget accounts.

Social Security Administration Categories

Yet another classification is that used by the Social Security Administration in the social welfare expenditure series. Since the 1950s the Social Security Administration has been publishing this series of federal, state, local, and private social welfare expenditures.[6] It is drawn from published and unpublished sources and is available for the period covering 1929–1980. This series is widely relied upon to describe the social welfare effort of the United States and to compare that effort with that of other nations. It is a useful series because of the uniformity of definitions and inclusion rules used over the years.

Despite the series' usefulness, several drawbacks exist. One is that over the past the series relied on many figures that were not publicly available but were provided by government agencies. In recent years there has been a tendency to use public figures which do not go into as much detail to separate program and administrative costs. A second problem is that the program detail has not been published by the Social Security Administration beyond fiscal year 1966. The detailed figures have been made available to various researchers but are not easy to obtain for the most recent years. The third problem is that the program categories used in the SSA series have not been revised over the last twenty years. During this period social welfare expenditures have undergone much change. Consequently, a category such as "Other Social Welfare" is today a very large category. Any use of the SSA series requires access to the unpublished figures and reclassification into categories which are more useful today.

The definitions for programs used in this study are necessarily hybrids. We generally follow the rules of the Social Security Administration for program inclusion, the *CFDA* descriptions for definitions, and the data from the federal budget and OMB sources for the expenditures of these programs.

The use of the *CFDA* program definitions provides a more discrete definition than the other sources. This definition is determined largely by the rule that components of programs which have distinct beneficiary groups should be classified separately. For example, the *CFDA* classification would show the social security (OASDHI) programs as consisting of the following programs: old age insurance for retirees; insurance for survivors; special benefits for persons over age seventy-two; disability insurance; and health insurance (part A and part B). Other classifications might combine one or two of these programs. Each is shown distinctly in the federal budget. Each has a different eligibility group.

Some programs in the *CFDA* have been excluded here. These were primarily programs for research, funding for post-graduate education, and other education training. Also excluded are guaranteed loans; direct loans are included. Another category excluded were all programs for Indians. The numbers of these separate programs in education, health, social services, and housing tend to distort some of the categories. Indian programs, unlike the others here, fall under the jurisdiction of the Interior committees. The creation of these programs usually followed the initiation of assistance for other recipients. Otherwise, the influences on Indian programs have been distinct from the other programs. A few classifications have been added for federal employee benefits which the *CFDA* excludes.

These *CFDA* classifications are used in the summary of the number of programs and the analysis of the initiation of new programs. Without this distinction it is impossible to determine when programs begin because Congress and the president are often adding new provisions and beneficiaries to existing programs. The *CFDA* classifications can also be used as a base to measure modifications in program eligibility and benefits. In a series formerly compiled by *Congressional Quarterly*, presidential requests were coded as policy recommendations.[7] The problem with indicators of this sort is that there are no uniform units to measure whether a given statement constitutes one recommendation or two because it affects different programs. With a program definition, this unit can be used as a base for examining presidential recommendations. For example, a recommendation to expand eligibility in a program can be classified as the initiation of new program if it results in one.

POLICY CLASSIFICATION

Any analysis of social welfare involves the choice of a classification for the various programs. Classifications are employed by policy makers to compare programs with similar characteristics, target groups, or goals. These classifications are used by analysts of policy making because policies with similar characteristics are presumed to evoke similar policy decision rules. The nature of the policy process in Congress involves the consideration by specialized committees. This specialization by Congress and the bureaucracy tends to reinforce differences by policy types. What effect this has on policy outcomes requires further examination.

The question of the effect of the separate consideration of

types of policy is an important one. We know that congressional committees have different political environments, reflect differences in members goals, and have differing relationships with their parent body.[8] The jurisdiction over social welfare programs is divided among congressional committees. We also know that there has been differential growth in types of social welfare policy.[9] Health expenditures and food stamps have grown rapidly in recent years but were not major expenditures just ten years previously. From a policy standpoint, it is important to analyze expenditures by policy type because different types have varying beneficiary groups and benefit conditions. From a political perspective, analysis by policy type is important because we are interested in whether political influences vary by policy type.

The effect of policy type on outcomes is suggested by diverse studies. There is empirical evidence from the comparative state research of the differences in political influences by policy type.[10] There is certainly evidence that the effects of economic factors vary with types of social welfare policy.[11] Differences may occur as well in the influence of political factors. At the national level, studies of congressional voting, for example, point to differences in congressional behavior by policy type.[12] Lowi's proposition that policy affects the process by which decisions are made has resulted in many studies which use his classification.[13] The distributive policy studies rely on the Lowi classification. What emerges from all of these studies is the importance of policy type as a direct or mediating policy influence. The questions of how to classify policy and how to measure its effect on policy outcomes are less definitively answered.

Three alternative classifications can be considered and compared. These are based on functional budget categories, the Social Security Administration social welfare series, and classification by characteristics of the form of assistance and beneficiaries. Each has its merits as a decision making and analytic classification. Each has been used in previous studies. No single classification is sufficient, for each helps explain changes in social welfare policy from a different perspective.

Budget Categories

The budget categories used in the executive budget and the congressional budget process organize social welfare expenditures into four functional groupings: income security; education, manpower, social services; health; and veterans' benefits.[14] Some variants on these four functional categories have been used since 1949.

The titles of these functional categories have changed about every ten years to reflect the changes in the budget. For example, the 1985 budget shows social security and Medicare in a separate functional account. Prior to this these funds were shown in income security and in health. The last major change previously was in fiscal 1976. As programs have grown, categories such as "Health, Labor, and Welfare" have been divided into health and income security.

While the names and descriptions of the functional categories have changed about every ten years, the content of these functional categories has been more variable. From year to year, programs will appear in different functional categories. One change made in the 1985 budget was to move military retirement from the defense category to the income security category. National Science Foundation funding formerly was in education but now is in a new category with research funding. The subfunctional categories have changed even more to reflect the inclusion of new programs.

In order to have uniform categories over the years, we have created one set of current functional categories and subcategories from the federal budget and placed all programs in these categories from 1949 to 1985. This provides comparable categories which have heretofore not been available. In addition, as a second series we use data from the Office of Management and

Budget which show all budget expenditures in the 1985 categories. The OMB publishes these in the budget annually for selected years.[15]

These two series are not completely compatible. Certain decisions we have made deviate from current OMB classifications. For instance, we exclude military retirement expenditures. We also exclude a subfunctional category of "Other Labor Services," which includes some NLRB and administrative expenses for the Department of Labor. The two series are very close in total expenditures and in the four major categories. There is always less than a 2 percent deviation in the average annual change figures. The series created from the executive budgets are used to show the difference between presidential requests and actual expenditures. These data are not available from the OMB series which shows only expenditures and not requests.

Data on presidential requests for functional categories are obtained from the annual federal budgets. The categories are not available in the usual source for congressional appropriations because Congress did not consider the budget by functional category. These categories are useful, however, because they represent an emphasis which the president placed on different policy goals. Presidential requests are needed as a decision indicator to see whether expenditures increased due to a presidential request, congressional action, or economic and demographic reasons.

While the president has been using functional categories since 1949, the Congress did not begin to use them until 1975. Congress enacts thirteen separate appropriations acts, each of which is handled by a separate congressional appropriations subcommittee. The president's functional budget categories are designed to show total federal effort toward various goals. These functional categories include programs from numerous agencies. For example, the income security category includes expenditures for food and nutrition (Agriculture); public assistance (Health and Human Services and Social Security Administration); retirement (Civil Service and Social Security Administration); unemployment insurance (Labor); and low energy assistance (Health and Human Services and Community Services Administration). With the enactment of Great Society programs in the mid-sixties, these agency lines often became blurred. Manpower and training programs, for example, were funded both from the Department of Labor and the Office of Economic Opportunity (OEO) budgets. The Work Incentive program included both Labor and HEW funds. Explaining funding for food and nutrition programs would require a separate treatise.

Congress never considered the programs in the comprehensive way presented in the budget. Each component existed in the separate agency budgets and was considered individually by the appropriate appropriations subcommittee. Only with the passage of the Congressional Budget Act of 1974 and the establishment of the House Budget Committee and the Senate Budget Committee did Congress begin to use the functional categories as guidelines in budgeting. The implications of this fragmented consideration are explored when differences in presidential and congressional social welfare priorities are considered. It is not possible to obtain congressional figures comparable to the presidential functional category requests. We can and do, however, analyze congressional action on some individual programs which comprise the budget functions.

One other advantage of using the presidential budget series is that each budget breaks spending requests into components which are funded out of existing budget authority and those components funded from proposed budget authority. Proposed budget authority involves new authorization needed to govern the appropriations requested in the budget. This budget figure is an indicator of presidential legislative activity and presidential interest in modifying existing entitlements. Entitlements can be modified only if presidents obtain new authority to alter existing laws.

The subfunctional budget categories are modified to create categories similar to those others have used in analyzing data from the Social Security Administration series. Robert Plotnick, for example, uses seven categories: cash, food, housing, education, manpower, social services, and health.[16] The main difference between his classification and the budget classification is that he includes veterans' benefits with other benefits of a similar type and not as a separate category. The classification used here corresponds closely to the subfunctional budget classification.

These different series will be used separately and together. We will use the subfunctional categories, the CRS programs, and the *CFDA* classification to extend the four budget categories. The hierarchy of the classification begins with the four budget categories and proceeds to the subfunctional categories, the budget accounts, and finally the *CFDA* programs. Table 4-1 shows the functional and subfunctional groupings as well as the congressional committee jurisdiction for the major programs.

Each of the series has a different advantage and illuminates aspects of social spending that another series obscures. The budget functional and subfunctional classifications show presidential initiative in creating new programs. This allows us to see how programs have grown and to separate growth from presidential recommendations from automatic growth. The CRS series highlights the major programs. The *CFDA* series resolves more easily the issue of program definition and provides information on who benefits, when programs were enacted, and who initiated the programs. The SSA series permits the easy separation of administrative expenditures from program benefits. It also provides uniform rules across time for the inclusion of programs in the social welfare series. In addition, for four selected programs for which appropriations exist, we compare presidential requests with congressional action to further separate congressional priorities from presidential priorities.

Classification by Type of Assistance

Another way used to classify policies is by type of assistance and beneficiary group. The most commonly used distinctions

TABLE 4-1
Social Program Summary with Functional and Subfunctional Budget
Categories and Congressional Committee Jurisdiction

Income Security

1. Social Insurance: Retirement and Disability
Social Security	Ways and Means[1]
Civil Service Retirement	Post Office and Civil Service
Railroad Retirement	Interstate and Foreign
	Commerce[2]

2. Public Assistance (Other Income Security)
Aid to Families with	Ways and Means[1]
Dependent Children	
Supplemental Security	Ways and Means[1]
Income	
Assistance to Refugees	Judiciary[3]
Low Income Energy	Energy and Commerce[2]
Assistance	

3. Food and Nutrition Assitance
Food Stamps	Agriculture[4]
Commodity Assistance	Agriculture[4]
School Nutrition Programs	Education and Labor[2]
Other Nutrition Programs	

4. Housing   Banking and Currency[5]
   Public Housing
   Direct Loan Programs
   Rural Housing Programs

5. Unemployment   Ways and Means[1]
   Compensation
   Regular
   Special and Extended
   Programs

Health

6. Health Care Services: Insurance and Medical Assistance
Medicare	Ways and Means[1]
Medicaid	Ways and Means[1]

   Health Research, Training, Planning, and Construction
   Public Health

Education, Manpower, and Social Services

7. Education   Education and Labor[2]
   Elementary and Secondary Education
   Other Aids to Education (Supporting State Services)

continued

TABLE 4-1 *(continued)*

Higher Education	
Vocational and Adult Education	
Science Education and Basic Research	
8. Manpower, Training, and Employment Programs	Education and Labor[2]
9. Social Services	
Public Assistance Social Services	Ways and Means[1]
Specialized Services	

Veterans' Benefits and Services

10. Veterans' Benefits	Veterans' Affairs
Income Security for Veterans	
Veterans Education and Readjustment Benefits	
Hospital and Medical Care	
Other Veterans Benefits and Service	

[1] In Senate, Finance Committee.
[2] In Senate, Labor and Public Welfare Committee.
[3] In Senate, Foreign Relations Committee.
[4] In Senate, Agriculture, Nutrition, and Forestry Committee.
[5] In Senate, Banking, Housing and Urban Affairs Committee.

are to separate cash from in-kind benefits and income tested (low income) from nonincome tested benefits.[17] In order to separate benefits into these types, it is necessary to have benefits at a program level similar to the *CFDA* or the SSA series. Many of the budget accounts include programs which provide different types of benefits to different groups. For example, the income security category includes social security, low income energy assistance, housing, and food benefits.

A variant on this classification organizes expenditures by beneficiary group. This involves classifications such as retirement benefits (aged), disability benefits (workers), unemployment (workers), welfare assistance (poor), and veterans' benefits. The variant permits the analysis of beneficiaries under the myriad of U.S. social welfare programs. This last categorical analysis is similar to that found in the *Special Analysis of the Budget* for selected years.[18]

In the past this type of analysis has been accomplished with Social Security Administration data.[19] In this study, we will use the OMB series of benefits to individuals. These benefits are classified as retirement and disability, public assistance benefits, unemployment, food and nutrition assistance, housing assistance, assistance to students, and veterans' benefits. These are the benefits which are paid directly to individuals by the federal government or by the state or local governments using federal funds. This series includes some administrative costs if they are part of the budget appropriation account. These administrative expenditures, however, only affect changes in the series in the early years. Expenditures soon become very large in relation to administrative costs, so that any changes are masked by benefit costs.

In part of the analysis of payments to individuals, we remove veterans' expenditures from the series. Veterans' benefits, while an important part of the federal social welfare effort, have a dynamic of their own which can distort other domestic social welfare series. Veterans' benefits decline in the late Truman and early Eisenhower administrations, then pick up and decline again as Korean War veterans receive benefits. In the late 1960s the Vietnam War brings another cycle into the series. In addition there are certain programs such as the National Service Life Insurance for which there have been no new beneficiaries since 1956. All expenditures in this program are determined by demographic factors as eligible veterans claim their benefits.

The overlapping nature of the classifications as well as the categorical nature of U.S. social welfare programs is revealed in Table 4-2. Each classification obscures some program differences. The income security programs, as classified by the budget, consist of programs which provide cash or in-kind benefits. These cash, food, and housing benefits are paid to retirees and disabled persons, their spouses, and dependents, and to recipients who qualify because of low income. U.S. social welfare

TABLE 4-2
Classifications of Social Welfare Policy

Functional Budget Classification	Subfunctional Classification	Eligibility Categories
Income Security	Insurance Public Assistance Food Housing	Age Disability Income Survivors/ Dependents Employment

Education,
  Manpower, and
  Social Services
	Education
	Manpower
	Social Services
		Student
		Unemployed
		Income

Health	Health Care Research and Construction Public Health	Age Income
Veterans	Income Security Education Housing Medical Care Other services	Military Service Survivors/ Dependents

programs have almost always conditioned eligibility on some categorical qualification such as age, employment, disability, or dependent children.

SOCIAL WELFARE FUNCTIONAL CATEGORIES

The basis of the alternative classifications may also be seen by examining more closely the programs which comprise the four budget categories. In the following discussion, differences in type, conditions, and targeted beneficiaries in the budget categories are discussed. This discussion also provides background for the subsequent analyses of policy differences.

Income Security

The income security programs as classified in the *U.S. Budget* are programs designed to "mitigate the loss of family income when the wage earner is no longer in the work force because of unemployment, retirement, disability, or death."[20] Table 4-3 illustrates the distribution of income security dollars in one year, 1981. The majority of cash benefits in Table 4-3 are insurance benefits conditioned on prior work history. Expenditures that are popularly termed "welfare" consist of Supplemental Security Income (SSI), Aid to Families with Dependent Children (AFDC), housing assistance, food stamps, and nutrition programs. The cash welfare programs are a very small portion of U.S. income security programs.

TABLE 4-3
U.S. Income Security Programs, FY1981

	Dollars[a] (in millions)	Percent
General Retirement and Disability[b]	$145,024	64.4%
Federal Employee Retirement and Disability	17,547	7.8
Unemployment Assistance	19,664	8.7
Other Income Security[c]	19,721	8.8
Housing Assistance	6,942	3.1
Food and Nutrition	16,202	7.2
Total	$225,100	100 %

[a]All figures are actual outlays in current dollars.

[b]Includes OASDI, railroad retirement, disability for coal miners (black lung).

[c]Includes SSI, AFDC, and refugee, energy, and emergency assistance.

Source: *Budget of the United States Government, Fiscal Year 1983.* Washington, D.C., Government Printing Office.

Education, Manpower, and Social Services

The second budget category consists of education, manpower, and social service programs. These programs are all designed to provide education, training, rehabilitation, employment, and social services to help persons become productive members of the labor force. One might term these programs investments in human capital.[21] They have been more recent additions to social welfare expenditures and grew most rapidly in the 1960s and early 1970s.

Health

Two programs, Medicare and Medicaid, currently comprise over 90 percent of the expenditures in the health policy category. Medicare provides payments for health care for the aged and disabled; Medicaid provides these benefits to low income persons. Both of these programs have only been in existence since the mid 1960s. Today they account for 15.6 percent of all U.S. social welfare expenditures.[22] The other health programs are categorical grants for maternal and child health and mental health and are relatively small in comparison. The health budget category also includes funding for health research. These funds are not included in the OMB payments to individuals series.

Veterans' Benefits and Services

Veterans have always enjoyed a special status in the design and delivery of U.S. social welfare programs. There are veterans' cash payments (pensions and compensation), housing benefits, education benefits, job training and rehabilitation benefits, and health benefits. These benefits may either be included in the respective policy categories described previously, or they can be analyzed separately. The separate treatment parallels their analysis in the *U.S. Budget* and by Congress and highlights the differences in the treatment of individuals under U.S. social welfare programs.[23] All veterans' benefit programs, regardless of the type of assistance, fall under the jurisdiction of the Veterans' Affairs committees. These committees consider housing, education, manpower, disability, and pension programs for veterans. Similar programs for nonveterans would fall under the jurisdiction of at least four different congressional committees. The incidence of war will influence veterans' benefits more directly than it influences other benefit programs and is another argument for their separate consideration.

The classification by condition of assistance (military service, physical impairment, low income) and by target groups (veterans, poor, retired) further illustrates the point that U.S. social programs should not be thought of as solely assistance to the poor. Furthermore, there are many strings attached to assistance. Social welfare expenditures consist of in-kind assistance, medical care, and aid programs to promote human and community development, as much as cash assistance. We will see later that cash programs have been expanded much more narrowly than have noncash programs.

This discussion reveals the diversity and conditional basis of our social welfare programs. The budget categories obscure many program differences. For example, the social insurance programs dominate the income security category but may have a different responsiveness to political and economic influences than do the in-kind income security expenditures. Alternative classifications are necessary to assess program differences.

The choice of policy category depends upon the question to be addressed. The budget categories are useful to analyze shares of the national budget directed toward the various functions. The functional distinctions can be broken down further as long as the relationship with the jurisdictional committees is retained. For example, including veterans' education benefits with all education expenditures ignores the fact that all veterans' benefits receive separate consideration by the veterans' committees and are not considered in the same manner as other education programs. We need to be able to separate the housing, food, and public assistance, and insurance programs within the income security functional category. However, in order to assess how well other target beneficiary groups have fared and whether policy expenditures for the poor, the aged, or children have had different periods of growth and policy influences, we need to use a beneficiary classification.

CONCLUSION

Therefore, a number of classifications beyond total expenditures will be used to assess the differential growth of U.S. social welfare policy. These are the functional budget categories and a refinement of the budget categories to show insurance, food, housing, and public assistance separately. This latter classification is similar to that used by Plotnick, but it keeps veterans' expenditures as a separate category. In addition, programs will be analyzed based on type of assistance (in-kind versus cash), condition of assistance (means tested versus nonmeans tested), and by beneficiary group. Finally, the average benefits of three major programs (social security, aid to families with dependent children, and the food stamp program) will be utilized.

In subsequent chapters we will see that social welfare programs have been expanded, conditions altered, new programs initiated, and benefits increased. These changes have been made in part in response to political and economic factors. The changes are also the result of both policy evolution and new approaches to eliminating poverty proposed by presidents, legislators, and academic scholars. The choices and emphases show up in the different growth rates of the categories of U.S. social welfare policy.

5

Social Welfare
Program Growth

THE NEW DEAL LEGACY

Most federal programs have their origin in the New Deal. Before that time, social welfare was a mix of state, local, and private efforts. While the role of the federal government has vastly changed and the size of the present federal programs dwarfs the modest New Deal beginnings, the basic shape and character of present-day programs still reflect much of this New Deal origin.

Very few changes were made in social welfare programs until after the Second World War. In the 1950s coverage under the social insurance programs was expanded. As the social insurance expenditures grew, veterans' expenditures declined. The social insurance component has expanded to the point where it now overshadows the other categories. The growth in the insurance and public assistance categories since 1970 is due in part to health expenditures which the Social Security Administration includes in these categories. If Medicare is moved from insurance and Medicaid from public assistance, the 1980 figures in Table 5-1 would show 50 percent in insurance, 11 percent in public assistance, and 20 percent in health.

In real terms, federal social welfare expenditures have at least doubled every decade.[1] The decade of the 1960s shows the largest real gains. The decade of 1970s reflects the effects of

TABLE 5-1
Federal Social Welfare Expenditures By Category
(in millions of current dollars)

	FY1950	FY1960	FY1970	FY1980
Social Insurance	$2,103.0	$14,307.2	$45,245.6	$191,106.9
Public Assistance	1,103.2	2,116.9	9,648.6	49,252.2
Veterans	6.386.2	5,367.3	8,951.5	21,253.6
Education	156.7	867.9	5,875.8	12,990.2
Health and Medical	603.5	1,737.1	4,775.2	13,348.0
Housing	14.6	143.5	581.6	6,608.1
Other	174.0	416.7	2,258.9	8,785.9
Total	$10,541.2	$24,956.6	$77,337.2	$303,344.9
Total in 1972 dollars	$18,924.9	$35,100.7	$85,361.1	$169,277.3

Federal Social Welfare Expenditures by Category as Percent of Total

	FY1950	FY1960	FY1970	FY1980
Social Insurance	20.0%	57.3%	58.5%	63.0%
Public Assistance	10.5	8.5	12.5	16.2
Veterans	60.6	21.5	11.6	7.0
Education	1.5	3.5	7.6	4.3
Health and Medical	5.7	7.0	6.2	4.4
Housing	0.1	0.6	0.1	2.2
Other	1.6	1.7	2.9	2.9
Total	100 %	100 %	100 %	100 %

All figures are in nominal dollars except as noted and include all administrative, construction, and research expenditures. Categories are those used by the Social Security Administration.

Source: Ann Kallman Bixby, "Social Welfare Expenditures, Fiscal Year 1980," *Social Security Bulletin* 46 (Aug. 1983):9–17.

inflation on expenditures which grew to over $300 billion. While expenditures have been increasing steadily since 1950, the annual percentage increases measured in 1972 dollars are much more variable. The real average rate of increase for fiscal years 1950 to 1984 is 6.9 percent.[2] Within these four-year averages annual changes range from a minus 12.7 to a positive 21.5

TABLE 5-2
Percent Change in Total Social Welfare Expenditures by Presidential
Administration, 1949–1977

President	FY	Years	Nominal Dollars	Real Dollars
Truman	49–53	5	4.0%	1.2%
Eisenhower	54–61	8	12.0	10.1
Kennedy	62–64	3	4.5	3.0
Johnson	65–69	5	14.6	11.4
Nixon	70–75	6	15.4	8.8
Ford	76–77	2	14.0	7.0
Carter	78–80	3	11.7	2.6

Note: Excludes all administrative, construction, and research expenditures. Includes administrative expenditures for Carter years.

Source: Calculations by author from Social Security Administration data.

percent. The percentage change figures do mask the increases in the size of federal expenditures as well as the relative size of the budget categories shown in Table 5-1. Percentage change figures are useful, however, in showing the increases from year to year in standardized units.

SOCIAL WELFARE SPENDING AND PRESIDENTIAL ADMINISTRATIONS

If the annual real percentage changes are calculated to show average changes over the presidential administrations, some interesting differences can be observed.[3] The percentage changes for social welfare have been much larger in the three Republican administrations than the four Democratic administrations with only one exception, the Johnson presidency. The rankings change somewhat if one considers changes in nominal expenditures, that is, expenditures which are not adjusted for inflation. This reflects the increases in inflation experienced in the early seventies during the Nixon and Ford presidencies. When considering real expenditure changes, however, the percentage increases in per capita spending for federal social welfare during the Eisenhower, Nixon, and Ford presidencies exceed that of the Truman, Kennedy, and Carter presidencies.

The larger increases observed in social spending during Republican administrations over Democratic administrations at first appears counterintuitive and against the popular wisdom that Democratic presidents promote social spending. This difference is even more apparent when one compares total budget outlays with the social program outlays in Table 5-3. While Republican presidents were successful in holding down total outlays and the nonsocial program components of the budget, they did not have the same impact on social spending. Growth in social programs exceeded the growth in the nonsocial components by at least five times in every Republican administration save one—the Reagan administration. Annual growth in social expenditures was less than 2 percent during the Reagan presidency.[4] The nonsocial components grew at 6.5 percent during this time reflecting the increases in the military budget. The Kennedy and Carter administrations look much the same. Spending for all programs is about at the same level and lower than the Republican administrations. The Johnson administration shows the impact of the emphasis placed on social spending.

Looking beyond these totals, the different priorities in social programs can be seen in the budget category percentage change figures. Table 5-3 also shows these differences for the four major social welfare budget categories. The Republican administrations show the largest increases in income security, which is composed of cash and in-kind benefits, both of which are means tested and nonmeans tested. The Reagan and Truman administrations are the exceptions to their party patterns. The Kennedy and Johnson administrations, which show smaller percentage change increases for income security programs, have much larger percentage increases for the in-kind categories: health and social services. These Democratic administrations had a different program emphasis from the preceding and follow-

TABLE 5-3
Real Annual Change in Budget Outlays by Presidential Administration, 1950–1985

	All Expenditures			Social Welfare			
President	Total	Non-Social Welfare	Social Welfare	Income Security	Education, Manpower, Social Services	Health	Veterans
Truman	16.0%	21.1%	1.6%	12.0%	23.4%	12.0%	−7.8%
Eisenhower I	−1.2	−3.6	9.7	15.1	7.6	8.9	1.0
Eisenhower II	4.4	2.0	11.3	14.5	14.1	15.5	1.5
Kennedy–Johnson	3.5	3.4	3.9	3.7	18.0	17.3	−1.2
Johnson	8.3	6.5	12.2	6.7	38.0	57.2	4.4
Nixon	3.1	−2.5	11.3	13.3	9.6	7.9	7.3
Nixon-Ford	4.6	1.0	8.2	8.6	5.4	11.5	2.7
Carter	4.0	4.5	3.7	4.0	2.1	6.5	−2.4
Reagan I	3.9	6.5	1.6	1.4	−7.0	6.5	−1.0

Note: Social welfare expenditures include all expenditures in income security, education, manpower, and social services, health, and veterans benefit functional categories. Trust funds are included. Reagan administration figures include four years.

Source: Calculations by author from OMB data.

ing Republican administrations. The Carter administration looks much more like the Republican administrations it falls between than the previous Democratic administrations. The changes in the veterans category reflect, in part, the cyclical effect of war efforts.

These snapshots of patterns of social spending suggest that popular wisdom about Democratic and Republican presidents is insufficient to understand how and when federal social spending has increased. It is necessary to look more closely at components of these budget categories since each level of aggregation hides variation. Large programs can easily dominate policy categories obscuring the creation of new, smaller programs. Budget decisions for agencies may follow different rules than budget decisions for programs. Decomposing these expenditures into categories that illuminate important policy choices and changes is an important first step to link these decisions to policy influences.

Understanding how these decisions were affected by policy influences is the next step in this process. These influences include the party of the president, the partisan composition of Congress, and the prevailing economic conditions. Most importantly, we need to be able to determine whether growth in social expenditures was the result of presidential priorities, whether it was the result of congressional actions, or whether this spending was driven by factors exogenous to the political process. Who has set the priorities for social spending is a central question for this analysis.

SOURCES OF PROGRAM GROWTH AND EXPANSION

Since the programs being described are predominately payments to individuals, increases in expenditures most often result from adjustments in eligibility conditions or benefit amounts. The following five causes underlie most social welfare expenditure increases. 1) new programs may be added; 2) benefit payments may be increased; 3) eligibility conditions may be modified in a way which affects program participation; 4) the federal share of program costs may be increased or federal program appropriations may be increased—this applies primarily to programs which require a state or local contribution or for programs in which funds are not appropriated or calculated on an individual basis; 5) expenditures may increase in response to economic conditions, demographic changes, and changes in household composition.

In the balance of this chapter growth in federal programs resulting from three of these five reasons is examined. We look at the enactment of new programs, increases in federal appropriations, and responsiveness to economic conditions. The intent is to separate congressional initiatives from presidential initiatives and to separate the effects of previous decisions from those of current decisions. In chapter six program growth by beneficiary group and program conditions is examined. In chapter seven we look specifically at increases in benefits and changes in eligibility conditions.

NEW PROGRAM INITIATIVES

Enumerating social programs is necessarily fraught with error. Using the *Catalog of Federal Domestic Assistance (CFDA)*, we have enumerated 177 programs which have been created in the post-war period. This figure does not include 30 programs which existed before 1946. Also excluded are research, training, and construction programs and loan guarantee programs. A program which has been reauthorized but not substantially changed is not counted as a new program unless it had a different target population or was split into different components. A presidential initiative is one which the president proposed in a message to Congress, in the budget, or other legislative message. A congressional initiative is one which is introduced by a member of Congress, added to a bill in committee, or amended into the bill on the floor. An action such as this to which the president agrees is still considered a congressional initiative. This enumeration is not designed to be the last word on the number of social programs, but to show presidential and congressional policy interest by policy category and beneficiary group.

The tabulation shown in Table 5-4 indicates program initiation using the *CFDA* data. Presidential and congressional initiatives number just about equal. Democratic presidential policy initiatives outnumber four times the Republican initiatives. Of the congressional initiatives, an equal number originate during same party control as during different party control of Congress and the presidency. In summary, however, we see that almost twice as many programs are initiated during periods of

TABLE 5-4
New Program Initiatives by President and Congress, 1947–1982

Conditions of Party Control	Initiated by President	Initiated by Congress	Total
Democratic President and Democratic Congress	75	41	116
Democratic President and Republican Congress	0	1	1
Republican President and Democratic Congress	16	41	57
Republican President and Republican Congress	2	1	3
Total	93	84	177

Source: Calculations by author from *CFDA* data.

Democratic control of the presidency and the Congress than during the combination of Republican presidencies and Democratic congresses. During Republican presidencies, the Democratic Congress initiates programs. During Democratic presidencies, the Democratic congresses are more restrained because of the increases in presidential initiatives. If a Democratic president does not propose many new programs, Congress will initi-

TABLE 5-5
Large Program Initiatives by President and Congress, 1947–1982

Conditions of Party Control	Initiated by President	Initiated by Congress	Total
Democratic President and Democratic Congress	8	0	8
Democratic President and Republican Congress	0	0	0
Republican President and Democratic Congress	1	4	5
Republican President and Republican Congress	0	0	0
Total	9	4	13

Source: Calculations by author from CRS data.

ate its own. This is seen in the Truman and Carter presidencies (see Table 5-6). During the Kennedy and early Johnson presidency, Congress followed the president. Beginning with Johnson's full term, we see an increasingly active Congress initiating social programs.

It should be noted that these figures do not in anyway reflect the size of programs. Some of these programs are very small. The figures do, however, reveal the specialization and diversification of the welfare state. For example, a program, such as unemployment benefits for displaced redwood workers, illustrates how eligibility and benefits have been defined in increasingly narrow terms to capture more in the social welfare net.

We can get a better sense of the importance of programs by examining the large program initiations. Using the CRS definition of programs costing over $1 billion in 1980 and constituting an OMB budget account, we find a pattern similar to that noted above. Nine of these programs were initiated by presidents; four by Congress. Eight of the nine presidential programs were initiated by Democratic presidents. Neither of these program classifications is satisfactory alone. The former includes many small components of large programs; the latter aggregates the many small components. The results of these different levels of program aggregation are very similar.

From the earlier discussion on the New Deal legacy, it should not be surprising to learn that very few cash programs have been enacted—only ten to be exact. These include social security benefits for those over age seventy-two, social security disability benefits, black lung disability payments, Aid to the Permanently and Totally Disabled, AFDC for unemployed parents, Supplemental Security Income, Emergency Assistance, two programs for Haitian and Cuban refugees, plus one new veterans' program. Excluded from this list are thirteen programs which provide extended unemployment benefits. In terms of big programs, there are just two: social security disability benefits and Supplemental Security Income. In contrast, there have been 167 new noncash programs enacted since 1945.

TABLE 5-6
New Programs by Policy and Initiator, 1946–1982

	Truman		Eisenhower		2		Kennedy		Johnson*		Johnson		Nixon		Nixon–Ford		Carter		Reagan**		Total	
	C	P	C	P	C	P	C	P	C	P	C	P	C	P	C	P	C	P	C	P	C	P
Insurance	1	0	1	0			0	3			1	0	1	0							3	5
Public Assistance											1	0	0	1	0	1	3	0			5	8
Employment	0	3	0	2	0	1	0	1	0	1	2	4	3	2	1	1	1	0			8	9
Food	4	0	1	0	2	0	0	1	1	0	0	7	5	0	0	1					7	9
Housing					0	1	0	2			3	7	2	0	2	0					7	10
Health							0	1	0	4	2	5	1	0	4	2	3	0	0	2	10	14
Social Services							1	2	0	4	5	5	1	1	5	0	2	4	1	0	15	16
Manpower	1	0			2	1	2	2	0	2	7	15	4	1	3	1					19	22
Education	2	0	2	0									1	0							5	0
Veterans	2	0																				
Total	8	3	4	2	4	3	3	13	1	11	21	44	18	5	15	6	9	4	1	2	84	93
Total Overall	11		6		7		16		12		65		23		21		13		3		177	

Key: C = Congressional initiative; P = Presidential initiative.
* Johnson's first year is shown separately.
** Reagan administration includes first two years only.

Cash programs are found in the insurance, public assistance, and veterans categories.

Source: Calculations by author from *CFDA* data.

The major federal cash programs, the social insurance and public assistance programs, predate the Second World War. These programs constitute 70 percent of the total federal payments to individuals in 1983. The new programs, especially in the areas of health and nutrition, have grown to be a major component of the overall social welfare effort. New health and nutrition components constitute an additional 23 percent of payments to individuals. The remaining 7 percent, or $28.1 billion, is in other programs.

Table 5-6 depicts the growth by time and by type of program. The post-War on Poverty growth is clearly evidenced. The pattern of presidential and congressional initiatives seen in Table 5-4 is also reflected within the subprograms. Presidential and congressional initiatives are just about equal. The exceptions are social insurance and veterans' benefits where all the initiatives have been congressional rather than presidential. After the enactment of the housing programs in the Truman administration, presidents have dominated housing program initiatives over Congress. One other notable exception occurs with unemployment compensation programs. This is the only category in which there have been more Republican presidential initiatives than Democratic. This results from the occurrence of recessions during Republican presidencies which have compelled Republican presidents to propose extensions of unemployment programs. Four of the 5 congressional employment initiatives have occurred during Republican presidencies. In marked contrast, of the 15 initiatives in manpower programs, 14 have been made by Democratic presidents.

The data in Table 5-6 indicate that Democrats have initiated the in-kind programs. This is seen in the food, social services, education, manpower, and health categories. The table also again shows how few new cash programs have been enacted. New cash programs have been added for extended unemployment benefits and for disabilities but rarely for other conditions of poverty.

NEW BUDGET AUTHORITY

In order to assess program growth in new and existing programs that arise from presidential initiatives, we can utilize an indicator available in presidential budgets since 1949. This is the dollar value of new legislation proposed by the president. Presidents must seek new authority for policy changes that go beyond the authority of the present statutes. All presidential budgets show authority and outlays under proposed and existing provisions. The new budget authority encompasses increases in program benefits, eligibility, federal share, and appropriations. It also indicates decreases recommended by presidents.[5] We use this indicator to show presidential policy preferences. Table 5-7 shows estimated outlays under proposed legislation for each post-war administration.

Democratic presidents have been more active in proposing new legislation to increase social spending than have Republi-

TABLE 5-7
Total Amount of New Outlays Recommended by Presidents in Annual
Budget Message, 1950–1985

	Total	Income Security	Education, Manpower, and Social Services	Health	Veterans Benefits and Services
Truman	$3,856.6	$1,331.0	$2,056.6	$189.5	$279.6
Eisenhower I	825.7	580.3	96.8	103.4	45.1
Eisenhower II	677.9	0.0	519.4	4.4	154.1
Kennedy	4,292.6	1,795.8	2,251.2	167.4	78.2
Johnson	8,110.0	8,159.4	−303.3	445.9	−192.1
Nixon	8,720.5	9,458.4	673.0	−1,737.8	326.8
Nixon–Ford	−10,829.6	−5,189.9	−354.3	−3,964.5	−1,321.0
Carter	3,434.2	−861.4	5,840.8	−2,175.3	630.1
Reagan I	−18,193.0	−11,699.7	−2,519.2	−4,562.2	588.1

Note: All figures in millions of 1972 dollars. Reagan administration includes four years.

Source: Calculation by author from executive budget data.

can presidents. Under the latter, requests for new spending authority are lower. Requests are negative in the second Nixon administration and the Reagan administration. All post-Johnson presidents sought to curtail spending for health programs. The negative figure in the education, manpower, and social service category during the Johnson administration arises from reductions in outlays due to a change in the college housing loan program. The $5 billion increase in this category during the Carter administration arises from new authority for manpower and jobs programs. The Nixon administration clearly stands out in contrast to the other Republican administrations. Nixon sought increased authority for retirement and disability programs as well as for public assistance programs.

Utilizing presidential recommendations for total budget outlays and actual outcomes, we can compare presidential requests with presidential success in receiving those requests.[6] These figures (see Table 5-8) reveal an interesting paradox of social welfare spending. While increases proposed under Democratic administrations generally exceed those recommended under Republican presidents, the actual increases observed are higher under Republican administrations. Either Democratic presidents are less successful in obtaining the increases and new legislation that they request or Congress gives the Republican presidents much more than they ask for. Actual expenditures are always less than forecast by Democratic presidents, except for the Republican-appearing Carter administration. The change in actual expenditures always exceeds the estimated change in expenditures forecast by Republican presidents. The result is an annual rate of growth in expenditures under the Eisenhower, Nixon, Ford, and Reagan administrations which exceeds that of the Truman, Kennedy, and the Carter administrations. The only Democratic president with an average increase equal to the Republicans administrations is Johnson. The real growth of 11.6 percent during the Johnson term is still much less than the requested 15.9 percent increase.

TABLE 5-8
Average Real Presidential Requests and Actual Outlays by Budget Category, 1950–1985

	Total Social Welfare		Income Security		Education, Manpower, Social Services		Health		Veterans	
	Request	Actual	Request	Actual	Request	Actual	Request	Actual	Request	Actual
Truman	6.6%	0.5%	20.2%	12.3%	266.7%	48.8%	39.4%	14.8%	−10.8%	−11.0%
Eisenhower I	4.9	9.8	7.1	15.0	3.6	2.1	9.6	10.1	0.9	1.3
Eisenhower II	0.4	12.8	−0.8	16.3	29.6	24.7	10.8	16.6	0.5	0.8
Kennedy	4.6	3.7	2.7	2.8	47.6	20.7	22.3	18.0	−1.1	0.4
Johnson	15.9	11.6	16.2	5.3	24.3	36.3	53.4	61.6	0.6	3.9
Nixon	5.5	11.7	7.0	13.8	1.9	9.0	5.0	8.4	2.2	9.1
Nixon–Ford	0.6	7.8	2.9	8.3	−4.9	5.9	1.2	10.6	−10.1	1.9
Carter	1.2	3.6	1.5	4.2	3.1	2.1	2.0	5.1	−4.4	−2.9
Reagan*	2.0	1.8	3.4	1.9	−17.1	−7.4	3.6	5.4	0.5	−1.4

* Reagan requests are based on estimated outlays FY84 since actual outlays are not available. Actual average is based on three years for Reagan.

Note: Requests are the percentage change in outlays requested in the president's current budget over actual outlays for the previous fiscal year. Actual indicates the percentage change in actual outlays for the current fiscal year over actual outlays for the previous fiscal year. All are averages over presidential administrations in real 1972 dollars.

Source: Calculations by author from executive budget data.

Yet another way to see the intended impact of presidents on social priorities is to examine the revised budgets which presidents submit following the election of a president of the opposite party. Presidential budgets are usually submitted by the outgoing president a week before the inauguration of the new president. The incoming president often transmits to Congress revisions to the pending budget requests. Presidents Kennedy, Nixon, Carter, and Reagan did this. President Eisenhower did not. President Truman, however, deliberately refrained from

TABLE 5-9
Real Changes in Estimated Outlays Recommended
by Incoming Presidents

	FY 62	FY 70	FY 78	FY 82
	Kennedy	Nixon	Carter	Reagan
Income Security				
Insurance	$−71.2	$0	$−148.3	$−1,456.3
Other Income Security	+308.2	$1.1	+659.7	−485.4
Food	+231.5	−61.8	+1,426.2	−1,504.8
Housing	+89.0	−57.4	+87.2	−48.5
Unemployment	+602.7	+26.5	−504.0	+728.2
Total	+1,160.2	−91.6	+1,487.2	−4,223.0
Education, Manpower, and Social Services				
Education	+746.6	−423.8	+337.6	−970.9
Manpower	0	−199.8	+4,261.0	−2,184.5
Social Services	+68.5	−77.3	+177.2	−679.6
Total	+595.0	−899.7	+4776.5	−3,834.0
Health	+93.1	−624.7	+938.9	−1,165.0
Veterans	+89.0	−78.4	+579.1	−388.5
Total	$+2,157.5	$−1,495.6	$+7776.6	$−9,611.6

Note: All are recommended outlay changes in 1972 dollars.

Source: Kennedy: House Document 87–120 (March 24, 1961). Nixon: House Document 91–100 (April 15, 1970). Carter: *Budget Revisions,* (GPO, Feb. 1977). Reagan: *Budget Revisions,* (GPO, March 1981).

submitting new proposals in his final budget. Presidents Carter and Reagan transmitted extensive revisions in separate budget books. Table 5-9 displays the changes made by the incoming presidents. These adjustments have been made in all the presidential request data presented.

The differences in presidential policy preferences are clearly apparent from this table. Democratic presidents favored increases in income security programs that are not work conditioned. These are the food, housing, and public assistance programs. They also supported increases in education, social services, and health. Democrats sought less for insurance programs. Reagan sought less for everything except unemployment. These changes must be viewed from the requests left by the outgoing president. Presidents Eisenhower and Ford were recommending very few increases in their last budgets. Thus, the Kennedy and Carter changes are to restore budget authority which was proposed to be cut in the pending budget.

BUDGET SUBFUNCTION DIFFERENCES

This pattern of Democratic and Republican policy differences is also seen by looking at the budget subfunctional categories. Table 5-10 breaks the income security category into its component parts: retirement, other income security, food, housing, and unemployment compensation. Retirement which is dominated by social security benefits shows larger real average increases during Republican administrations than during Democratic administrations. It is the one category in which President Eisenhower sought increases. Other income security—which includes public assistance payments, Supplemental Security Income, refugee assistance, and in later years low income energy assistance—also has grown more during Republican administrations than during Democratic administrations. These gains are in the opposite direction of presidential intent. The second Eisenhower administration and the Nixon-Ford administration

TABLE 5-10
Presidential Requests and Actual Outlays for Income Security, 1950–1985

	Retirement		Other Income Security		Unemployment		Food	
	Request	Actual	Request	Actual	Request	Actual	Request	Actual
Truman	73.0%	29.3%	12.4%	7.1%	-24.8%	0.4%	-3.0%	0.0%
Eisenhower I	11.8	20.4	-3.5	2.5	-5.6	13.9	-10.4	3.2
Eisenhower II	7.1	13.9	1.1	6.5	-28.8	39.0	-17.4	24.7
Kennedy	5.2	6.8	7.8	5.7	-10.4	-13.0	25.7	4.3
Johnson	18.2	7.3	7.9	3.8	9.1	-9.5	15.2	14.7
Nixon	7.2	12.3	16.3	9.7	-10.4	24.6	22.0	48.9
Nixon–Ford	4.0	6.4	-0.9	11.9	3.1	26.8	-9.4	22.3
Carter	3.3	4.4	-2.0	4.4	-6.7	2.1	-4.8	8.2
Reagan*	8.0	4.5	-9.6	-1.7	-7.9	20.3	-14.9	0.5

* Reagan requests are based on three years; actual outlays are based on two years.

Note: Requests are the percentage change in outlays requested in the president's current budget over actual outlays for the previous fiscal year. Actual indicates percentage change in actual outlays for the current fiscal year over actual outlays for the previous fiscal year. All are averages over presidential administrations in real 1972 dollars.

Source: Calculations by author from executive budget data.

show efforts to reduce expenditures with little effect. The first Nixon administration and the first budget of the second term recommended increases as part of the welfare reform effort. The subsequent recommendations of this term were all negative. Expenditures grew 12 percent nonetheless. The largest real increases in other income assistance are observed during the Nixon and Ford administrations. The original War on Poverty programs were not directed at cash payments to eliminate poverty. Instead the emphasis was on community services, manpower, and education programs. The growth during the Johnson years shows up in the education, manpower, and social service category and in health. Johnson did, however, recommend social security benefit increases.

Expenditures in the food category show an interesting twist. While Democrats generally sought larger increases than Republicans, actual increases are larger during Republican administrations than during Democratic. Nixon was the exception among the Republicans. He sought large increases in the food program and made it a national program. Carter sought to cut expenditures in this program but succeeded only in slowing its real rate of growth.

Party differences appear the greatest in the unemployment compensation subfunctional category. Average real program growth is over 10 percent in every Republican administration but is only above zero in one Democratic administration. All of these Republican presidents were estimating lower expenditures, indicating that the economic downturns were bigger than was anticipated.

Several dominant findings can be seen in the analysis thus far. The growth in social spending which expands at a greater rate during Republican administrations results primarily from retirement and unemployment programs. Democrats have favored in-kind over cash programs. Growth in many programs has occurred during Republican administrations.

What might help explain this puzzling finding? Is it simply that unemployment drives federal spending up during Republican administrations? Have Democratic presidents been less successful in increasing social spending than Republicans? How do we reconcile the Democratic program initiation with the growth observed during Republican administrations?

ECONOMIC CONDITIONS

There is no question that expenditures have risen during Republican administrations because of recessions which have occurred during these periods. The 1985 federal budget describes this effect.

Higher unemployment leads directly to higher unemployment benefits with almost no lag. It also raises outlays for certain other programs, such as social security, food stamps, and public assistance, which have more beneficiaries when unemployment rises. Outlays for the latter programs generally increase with some lag. A one percentage point rise in the unemployment rate would add an estimated $4.9 billion to 1985 outlays with about two-thirds of the increase being for unemployment benefits.[7]

Unemployment decreased throughout the Truman, Kennedy, and Johnson terms but increased during the second Eisenhower term and the Nixon and Ford terms (see Figure 5-1). The rate was stable during the first Eisenhower term. Unemployment was increasing during the Carter administration and declined in the latter part of the first Reagan term. These three administrations are exceptions to the rule of observing increasing unemployment during Republican administrations and decreasing unemployment during Democratic administrations.

PRESIDENTS AND CONGRESS

This emphasis on presidential recommendations and policy priorities neglects the important observation that the Congress

FIGURE 5-1
Fluctuations in Unemployment, FY 1950-1985

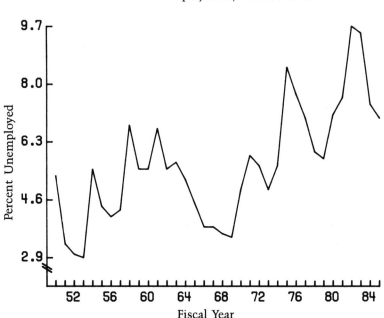

Source: *Economic Report of the President, 1985*
Note: Unemployment as percent of civilian labor force.

may have its own agenda for policy which may diverge from the president's. Throughout most of the period in question Congress has been controlled by Democrats. Congress generally ignored Republican proposals to cut expenditures. This is especially true of the Eisenhower and Ford recommended cuts. Truman and Kennedy fared much worse with their proposals to increase social spending. Even under Johnson, expenditures did not increase at the level he proposed and estimated. Nixon's expansions were enacted and added to. In chapter seven we look more closely at how Congress outbid the president on social security benefits during Republican administrations.

Table 5-11 shows the ratio of the presidents' estimated expen-

TABLE 5-11
Actual Budget Outlays as a Percent of Presidential Budget Requests, 1950–1985

	Truman	Eisenhower I	Eisenhower II	Kennedy	Johnson	Nixon	Nixon–Ford	Carter	Reagan*
Income Security	95%	107%	117%	100%	91%	106%	105%	103%	103%
Education, Manpower, Social Services	41	99	101	82	113	107	112	99	112
Health	80	100	110	100	110	100	111	100	100
Veterans	100	100	100	100	100	110	110	100	100
Total	95%	105%	112%	99%	96%	106%	107%	102%	103%

* Reagan average based on three years using estimated outlays for FY84.

Source: Author's calculations from executive budget data.

ditures and the actual expenditures.[8] It is generally less than or equal to 100 percent for Democrats and greater than 100 percent for Republicans. Democrats received a smaller percentage of the requests than did Republicans. Democrats usually requested more than Republicans, so expenditures might still be increasing. Actual outlays under Truman, Kennedy, and Johnson were less than these presidents estimated they would be. Congress ignored many of Carter's proposed cuts, and thus his percentage is closer to that of the Republicans. The figures show that Eisenhower's recommendations to cut income security programs, mostly public assistance, were ignored. They also show that Congress did not increase income security outlays as much as requested by Truman and Johnson. Kennedy's were on average equal to his requests.

The education, manpower, and social service category shows divergences as well. The Truman, Kennedy, and Carter estimated outlays are lower than actual outlays, while Johnson's are larger. Expenditures increased more in this category than recommended by Johnson. Expenditures exceed the proposed cuts in the Nixon, Ford, and Reagan administrations. While outlays exceeded estimates in the first two years of the Reagan term, average outlays for this category did decline 7.1 percent in real terms over the first three years.

Entitlements are not appropriated as are other annual programs. Consequently, we cannot obtain presidential requests and appropriation figures for all programs. Three selected programs which had annual appropriations are shown below. These programs represent a cash public assistance program, an in-kind other income security program, and all appropriations for education programs. The table show Democratic presidents receiving less than requested for the cash public assistance program. Republicans usually received what they requested. Interestingly, no Congress is championing the cause of public assistance. Increases are simply equal to or less than that requested. The largest increase occurs in the Nixon administration, and it was requested by Nixon.[9]

TABLE 5-12

Appropriations as a Percent of Presidential Budget Requests, 1950–1980

	Truman	Eisenhower I	Eisenhower II	Kennedy	Johnson	Nixon	Nixon–Ford	Carter*
Public Assistance	94%	100%	99%	93%	98%	100%	98%	98%
School Lunch	103	116	125	101	101	101	100	98
Education	93	100	109	97	105	99	123	102

* Carter calculations based on three years (FY78–FY80).

Source: Calculations form annual Senate Appropriations Committee summary document.

Requests versus Appropriations for Selected Programs, 1950–1980

		Truman	Eisenhower I	Eisenhower II	Kennedy	Johnson	Nixon	Nixon–Ford	Carter*
Public Assistance	Request	10.5%	6.9%	11.9%	14.5%	15.9%	22.0%	2.8%	10.2%
	Actual	4.5	6.6	10.4	6.3	13.4	22.0	0.7	6.7
School Lunch	Request	-2.7	-10.6	-9.6	-7.1	24.3	22.5	41.1	-3.1
	Actual	0.1	3.4	10.6	-6.3	24.2	23.6	41.2	-4.6
Education	Request	129.0	-3.4	159.8	78.4	35.8	2.9	-12.3	15.4
	Actual	121.4	-3.7	186.7	59.3	38.3	-2.5	10.3	19.0

* Carter calculations based on three years (FY78–FY80).

Note: Requests are the percentage change in appropriations requested in the president's current budget over actual outlays for the previous fiscal year. Actual indicates the percentage change in actual outlays for the current fiscal year over actual outlays for the previous fiscal year. All are averages over presidential administrations in real 1972 dollars.

Source: Calculations from annual Senate Appropriations Committee summary document.

Congress ignored President Eisenhower's request to cut school nutrition funds, went along with some of Kennedy's decreases, and followed the annual recommendations of Johnson, Nixon, and Ford. Carter succeeded in stopping some of the large increases in this program.

Funding for Special Milk, also a food program, was contained in another budget category. Presidents Nixon and Ford both recommended eliminating the Special Milk program, but Congress resisted. Carter recommended cutting over 80 percent of the Special Milk appropriation in two of his first three budgets. These recommendations were ignored as well. The program was finally eliminated in the Reconciliation Act of 1981.

Education appropriations show a mixed pattern. Truman and Kennedy received less than requested, Johnson and Carter slightly more. The first Eisenhower administration shows a decrease, but the second signals the beginning of a federal effort in education. The Johnson-Nixon transition shows a break with the Johnson emphasis on education spending. Expenditures increase again during the second Nixon term, despite the Nixon and Ford interest in cutting expenditures.

Assessing the effect of program lags is one of the more difficult issues in analyzing social program expenditures. Some of the increases observed from FY 1970 to 1977 result from decisions made during the Johnson years. The Elementary and Secondary Education Act resulted in increased education expenditures. Additional programs expanded aid for college education. Following the enactment of Medicare and Medicaid, expenditures for health were influenced by exogenous factors such as physician and hospital charges and the demand for medical care. With nutrition and manpower programs the post-War on Poverty increases observed in these programs result from presidential and congressional decisions during the Ford and Nixon years.

Few new programs were enacted during the Carter administration. While total expenditures continued toward new heights, the annual growth figures were much lower. This slowdown in growth and concern about program uncontrollability set the stage for the reductions enacted in the Reagan administration. The reductions enacted in 1981 were aimed at cutting back on many of the program expansions made in the 1970s.

ENTITLEMENTS AND UNCONTROLLABLE SPENDING

A large portion of federal domestic spending and the programs we are examining are termed uncontrollable and consist of entitlements. Entitlements are programs for which the beneficiary has a statutory claim to federal payments. Entitlements do not require congressional appropriations. Instead, costs are estimated and added into the budget. The federal government has through previous acts committed itself to pay benefits to all persons who meet the criteria specified in the law. The level of benefits is usually determined by a statutory formula. Entitlements constitute about half of the federal budget and are nearly two-thirds of all uncontrollable spending.[10]

The term uncontrollability was first used by the Office of Management and Budget in the 1971 budget to classify outlays which were for "open ended programs and fixed costs" and for "outlays from prior year contracts and obligations."[11] In addition to entitlements to individuals, uncontrollable expenditures include grants to states, General Revenue Sharing, and contractual obligations. Unlike other government expenditures, uncontrollable expenditures cannot be changed via the appropriations process. The government is obligated by law to spend fixed amounts that can only be modified by altering the authorizing language.

Of the total budget 37 percent is spent on retirement, unemployment, and medical entitlements amounting to $216 billion in fiscal 1980. Seventeen social programs are classified as entitlements. Six of these programs can be considered new entitlement programs; the others are New Deal social insurance and veterans' programs. The new programs include the three health

TABLE 5-13
Relatively Uncontrollable and Relatively Controllable Budget Outlays and Percent of Total Outlays in 1980
(in billions of current dollars)

Relatively Uncontrollable

Open-Ended Programs and Fixed Costs
Entitlements to Individuals

Social Security and Railroad Retirement	$121.8	21.0%
Federal Employees' Retirement	27.2	4.7
Unemployment Assistance	18.0	3.1
Medical Care	49.0	8.5
Assistance to Students	3.9	0.7
Veterans Compensation and Pensions	11.0	1.9
Food and Nutrition Assistance	13.2	2.3
Public Assistance and Related Programs	15.0	2.6
All other	3.1	0.5
Total	$262.2	45.3%
Other Entitlements	$6.8	1.2%
General Revenue Sharing	2.9	0.5
Social Service Grants	2.8	0.5
Total	$12.5	2.2%
Total Entitlements	$247.7	47.5%
Other Open-ended Programs and Fixed Costs*	15.7	2.7
Net Interest	52.5	9.1
Total Open-ended Programs and Fixed Costs	$342.9	59.3%
Outlays from Prior Year Obligations and Contracts	96.5	16.6
Total Relatively Controllable	$439.4	75.8%
Relatively Controllable	$146.0	25.2%
Undistributed Employer Share, Employee Retirement	−5.8	−1.0
Total Budget Outlays	$579.6	100.0%

*Includes housing assistance, Postal Service subsidy, and the legislative and judicial branches.

Source: GAO, "What Can Be Done to Check the Growth of Federal Entitlement and Indexed Spending?" March 3, 1981, p. 11.

care programs (Medicare parts A and B and Medicaid), social service grants to states, guaranteed student loans, and child nutrition programs. All but the child nutrition programs were enacted in the 1960s. The child nutrition programs were enacted as school lunch programs in 1946 and were given entitlement status in 1975.

Some classify food stamps as an entitlement; others have called it a *de facto* entitlement.[12] The following GAO explanation provides the basis for its decision to classify food stamps as an entitlement. This explanation suggests that what we term the program is less important than how decisions affecting the program are made.

> The entitlement status of the Food Stamp program is questionable. The Food and Agriculture Act of 1977 capped the overall funding level of the program and required that the program be funded through advance appropriations, thus removing the entitlement status. However, the Congress has continued to fund the program at the full level needed to provide stamps to all eligible people who apply; therefore the Congress still treats the program as a mandatory expenditure.[13]

There was a brief period in which food stamps were given an open-ended appropriation. It has never had a permanent authorization, however, and now is back to an annual, definite appropriation status.[14] Regardless of what the appropriation was termed or for what term it was appropriated, Congress always granted the necessary dollars to meet the demand. In 1981 the Reconciliation Act modified eligibility criteria to reduce expenditures. Whether an entitlement or not, food stamps grew like the genuine entitlements during the 1970s.

These social welfare entitlements have grown a great deal in the last fifteen years (see Table 5-14). Certainly much of this growth was due to inflation during the seventies. The Office of Management and Budget uses the following rules of thumb to estimate the budgetary impact of economic changes. A one percent change would increase indexed program costs $1.2 billion. A 1 percent increase in unemployment would increase unem-

TABLE 5-14
Growth in Selected Entitlement Programs
(in billions of current dollars)

	FY 70	FY 80	FY 82
Social Security			
Old Age Survivors	$26.7	$101.8	$140.3
Disability	2.9	15.3	19.4
Federal Employees' Retirement	5.8	27.3	36.6
Railroad Retirement	1.6	4.7	5.8
Unemployment	3.4	18.0	24.1
Medicare	7.0	35.0	46.6
Medicaid	2.7	14.0	18.1
Aid to Families with Dependent Children	4.1	7.3	7.7
Supplemental Security Income	0	6.4	8.0
Food Stamps	0.6	9.1	12.2
Child Nutrition	0.3	3.4	5.4
Social Service Grants	0.6	2.8	3.1
Veterans' Compensation and Pensions	5.3	11.0	13.7
Veterans' Readjustment Benefits	1.0	2.4	1.7
Disabled Coal Miners	0	1.8	2.0

Source: GAO, "What Can Be Done to Check the Growth of Federal Entitlement and Indexed Spending?" March 3, 1981, p. 18.

ployment and related programs by $4.9 billion for the same period.[15] It would be a mistake, however, to conclude that these programs are beyond control or that the hands of Congress and the president were tied permitting them only to watch with horror as federal spending increased.

Uncontrollability is a misnomer which serves to obscure the decisions and nondecisions made in the budget process. No program is beyond congressional control if Congress chooses to change the authorizing statute. The Reconciliation Act of 1981, the Social Security Amendments of 1977, and the social security changes of 1983 are very recent examples of congressional action to modify statutes which determine entitlement spending. The negative figures recommended by presidents as reductions in outlays in proposed legislation are further evidence of presidential interest in reducing uncontrollable outlays. These negative numbers stand out for Republican presidents in Tables 5-7 and 5-9.

For most of the period, food, housing, and education expenditures were neither uncontrollable nor entitlements. There is no denying the figures which show that Republican presidents were much more successful in controlling discretionary outlays than expensive social insurance outlays. Many of the changes which drove these expenditures higher, however, were discretionary additions to social insurance programs whose costs and benefits did not fall at the same time or on the same persons. Presidents Truman and Eisenhower recommended expanded coverage under social security. President Kennedy supported social security to persons over seventy-two not otherwise entitled and insurance benefits for jobs lost through foreign competition. Before allowing indexing for social security, benefits were increased 20 percent. All of these were additions or modifications to the statutes which changed formulas or entitled new beneficiary groups. The indexing provisions, which are certainly widespread in the budget today, arrived late in the game. The statutory provisions providing benefits and eligibility were already in place and had been put there by discretionary actions of the president and the Congress.

CONCLUSION

During Republican administrations the mainstay programs of the New Deal have been expanded. These are social security, public assistance, and unemployment. The innovations and creation of new programs have arisen during Democratic administrations. These programs are subsequently expanded by the Democratic congresses during the Republican administrations. Efforts of Republican presidents to reduce expenditures were usually thwarted by the Democratic congresses.

All presidents have been active in seeking new legislative

authority to affect entitlements and existing programs. These changes and the modifications added by Congress have resulted in the different rates of growth observed across the programs and the administrations. These periods of growth have also affected payments to the beneficiary groups who are the recipients of the social welfare programs.

6

Who Benefits

The categorical nature of social welfare policy and its differential growth in the United States has implications for the distribution of benefits. Federal social policy has mostly been indirect in its efforts to eliminate poverty. An individual may receive benefits from multiple programs, each having a different target population and eligibility conditions. Or, an individual might not qualify for any benefits if he or she slips through gaps in the eligibility categories. Examining spending by beneficiary group forces us to adopt categories which are, in part, artificial. These categories suggest a more comprehensive approach to policy-making than may actually exist. Programs are enacted individually and are under the jurisdiction of many different congressional committees. In this analysis programs are combined by eligibility criteria and beneficiary group. The categories place the emphasis on program impact.

THE DISTRIBUTION OF FEDERAL BENEFITS

The New Deal established social insurance as the dominant form of federal income security. These employment conditioned programs—social security, unemployment insurance, and disability insurance—are still the major components of federal social welfare spending. The public assistance categories were the residual groups. In time, more and more of the aged and the disabled were made eligible for the insurance benefits leaving intact poor families the major uninsured category.

The primary beneficiary groups of federal programs are the retired, unemployed, disabled, veterans, and the poor. The retired group was expanded to encompass spouses, widows, and the elderly poor. The unemployed group expands and contracts, but their benefits have always been tied to previous covered employment. Veterans are a special group. Every program which exists for others exists separately for veterans. This includes education benefits, pensions, disability, health, housing, and rehabilitation. Programs for the poor are primarily in-kind rather than cash.

For fiscal years 1970 to 1977, a period in which social programs were expanding, the Office of Management and Budget published annual figures which show expenditures by beneficiary group. These figures (Table 6-1) indicate that in 1970 three quarters of the income security dollars were paid to annuitants, aged, disabled, and unemployed. By 1977 this figure was over 80 percent. Funds going to those who are not in an insured category are small and have declined in proportion to the other categories.

The elderly stand out as the largest group other than veterans who receives benefits not based on previous employment. Benefits counted in the other aged category include spouses' and widows' benefits under the retirement programs as well as public assistance, food, housing and health benefits. In 1967, 57 percent of all cash benefits went to the elderly including aged annuitants. In addition, the aged received 68 percent of all in-kind income security benefits. This in-kind figure declined in subsequent years as other in-kind benefits to the nonelderly expanded, but the cash share remained around 60 percent.

Throughout these periods the federal government has tried many different indirect mechanisms to aid those who are simply poor. These efforts have included education, health care, food, housing, training, counseling, and occasionally cash pay-

TABLE 6-1
Federal Income Security by Beneficiary Group, 1970–1977

	FY1970	FY1974	FY1977
Annuitants	28.6%	28.6%	30.2%
Other Aged	33.1	30.5	29.9
Disabled	13.7	15.1	16.4
Mothers and Children	8.3	7.7	5.1
Temporary Unemployed		5.0	7.6
Transitional Low Income	9.2	7.3	5.4
Other	7.1	7.3	5.4
Total	100 %	100 %	100 %
Total (millions in current dollars)	$60.2	$111.2	$179.7

Source: *Special Analysis of the Budget,* 1972, 1976, 1979.

ments. Unlike the target groups of the elderly, the insured unemployed, the veterans, and the disabled, the poor are a difficult group to identify. They are the residual category. Many who would otherwise be poor are removed from poverty by the social insurance programs.

During the late 1960s, following Johnson's declaration of the War on Poverty, federal outlays directed toward the poor doubled. The growth in these outlays was not as large in the cash programs as it was in in-kind assistance. In-kind income security increased eight times while cash income security did not even double. Growth in the education, health, and other categories showed increases comparable to the in-kind income security growth. The growth in these targeted programs began to slow in the early seventies, but the growth of in-kind income security programs continued.

LOW INCOME PROGRAM INITIATION

The impact of the Johnson years can also be seen through an examination of initiations of low income programs. The enact-

TABLE 6-2
Outlays for the Poor, 1966–1971
(in billions of current dollars)

FY	Income Security			Education	Health	Manpower	Other	Total
	Cash	In-kind	Total					
1966	$8.1	$0.3	$8.4	$0.5	$0.8	$0.9	$0.5	$11.3
1967	8.3	0.3	8.6	0.9	2.1	1.2	0.7	13.5
1968	9.0	0.4	9.4	1.1	3.1	1.4	0.9	15.9
1969	9.8	0.6	10.4	1.1	3.6	1.4	0.9	17.5
1970	10.7	1.1	11.8	1.2	4.1	1.5	1.2	19.7
1971	13.2	2.4	15.6	1.5	5.0	1.9	1.5	25.5

Source: *Special Analysis of the Budget*, 1973.

ment of low income programs actually predates Johnson; President Kennedy initiated nine new income tested programs. These were spread across all categories: public assistance, health, social services, manpower, food, housing, and education. Of the thirteen new social programs initiated by Kennedy, nine were low income programs. The Johnson presidency accelerated this effort. Ten low income programs were initiated by Johnson in the year following Kennedy's death. This was followed by twenty-nine in the next four years.

Congress created its share of programs as well. Congress, which had followed the early lead of Kennedy and Johnson and had, in fact, resisted many of these programs in the late 1950s and early 1960s, created fifteen programs itself during the Johnson term. The congressional interest in new or revised low income programs continued in the 1970s after presidential interest waned. Program expansion continued during the post-Johnson years, but it was with a different emphasis.

Overall during the post-war period, Democratic presidents and the combination of Democratic presidents and Democratic Congresses are the conditions which fostered new programs. The differences are more striking than those seen with all programs. Only 8 low income programs out of the 103 were initiated by Republican presidents. This constitutes 44 percent of

TABLE 6-3
Initiation of New Income Tested Programs, 1947–1981

Conditions of Party Control	Initiated by President	Initiated by Congress	Total
Democratic President and Democratic Congress	52	29	81
Republican President and Democratic Congress	8	14	22
Total	60	43	103

Source: Calculations by author from *CFDA* data.

the 18 programs initiated by Republican presidents over the entire period. By comparison, 69 percent of the Democratic program initiatives have been low income tested programs. These same percentages apply when considering the programs initiated by the Congress. Seventy percent of the programs initiated during Democratic control of Congress and the presidency have been directed toward the poor. Only 34 percent of the programs initiated during Republican control of the presidency and Democratic congresses have been low income programs. The Democratic presidents, Kennedy and Johnson, set the agenda for programs for the poor.

CHANGES IN PAYMENTS TO INDIVIDUALS, 1950–1985

Using OMB data we can examine in more detail how programs which pay benefits to individuals have changed. This series is found in every budget and shows direct and grant-in-aid payments to individuals. The series pulls together data from all agencies in the budget. This classification includes all expenditures in an appropriation account "that are essentially income transfers in cash or in-kind to individuals or families and for which no current service is rendered."[1] The most notable programs excluded here are public service employment and man-

TABLE 6-4
New Low Income Programs by Policy and Initiator, 1947–1982

	Truman		Eisenhower I		Eisenhower II		Kennedy		Johnson*		Johnson		Nixon		Nixon–Ford		Carter		Reagan**		Total	
	C	P	C	P	C	P	C	P	C	P	C	P	C	P	C	P	C	P	C	P	C	P
Insurance																					0	0
Public Assistance	1	0					0	3			1	0	0	1	0	1	3	0			5	5
Employment							0	2	0	1	1	2	1	0	2	0					3	0
Food					1	0	0	1	1	0	0	7	4	0							5	4
Housing	3	0			0	1	0	1			2	5			0	1					5	9
Health							0	1			2	5									2	7
Social Services							0	1	0	4	2	3			2	2	2	0	0	1	6	13
Manpower							1	1	0	4	4	3			2	0	2	4			8	12
Education					1	0			0	1	5	7									8	10
Veterans			1	0									1	1							1	0
Total	4	0	1	0	2	1	1	9	1	10	15	29	6	2	6	4	7	4	0	1	43	60
Total Overall	4		1		3		10		11		44		8		10		11		1		103	

Key: C = Congressional initiative; P = Presidential initiative.
*Johnson's first term shown separately.
**Reagan's first two years only.

Source: Calculations by author from *CFDA* data.

power programs. This classification is essentially all of the income security programs, the veterans' income security programs, the veterans' readjustment (education) benefits, health care services, and the student assistance payments in education. The 1985 budget includes military retirement under income security for the first time and OMB has adjusted all of its figures to reflect this historically.

These figures once again show growth during Republican administrations and the Johnson administration. There is little difference between average real increases in the Eisenhower, Johnson, and Nixon administrations. The increases begin to decline under President Ford and continue downward through the Reagan administration. Again, the Truman and Kennedy administrations show the smallest average annual real increases. For the fiscal years from 1967 through 1985, it is possible to separate the controllable aspects of these expenditures. Controllable expenditures rose more than uncontrollable expenditures in the Johnson, Nixon, and Carter administrations. During the Ford and Reagan administrations, discretionary expenditures increased at a lower rate.

Other differences can be seen by looking at the components of payments to individuals. Unemployment payments demonstrate sharp differences between Democratic and Republican administrations. The Carter administration shows increasing costs of unemployment benefits toward the end of the administration; the Reagan administration shows the opposite trend. Expenditures increase at the beginning of the term and decline toward the end.

Retirement benefit growth, including social security, federal retirement, and military retirement, are greater than 10 percent in real terms in the Truman, Eisenhower, and Nixon administrations. Again, we see the Democratic administrations at a lower level of increases and the slowing down of increases beginning in the Ford administration. This growth is due in part to increases in social security benefits during these periods.

Public assistance shows a similar pattern of growth. The

TABLE 6-5
Average Real Changes in Payments to Individuals by Presidential Administration and Policy Category, 1950–1985

	Truman	Eisenhower I	Eisenhower II	Kennedy	Johnson	Nixon	Nixon–Ford	Carter	Reagan I
All	1.8%	10.0%	11.3%	3.2%	11.0%	11.8%	8.5%	4.1%	2.4%
Controllable					11.1%	21.0%	7.0%	7.6%	−1.4%
Uncontrollable					8.4%	10.8%	8.8%	3.7%	2.9%
Retirement	15.8%	14.6%	11.1%	6.7%	7.7%	11.1%	6.5%	4.1%	2.5%
Unemployment	1.0	17.6	34.1	−13.6	−4.4	20.8	28.7	2.1	−0.7
Public Assistance	7.4	4.3	8.1	4.6	2.5	6.2	8.0	0.7	−3.7
Food and Nutrition	−0.2	2.9	25.2	4.6	14.7	56.0	15.2	8.0	−3.1
Housing Assistance	69.9	36.9	12.3	7.6	8.5	41.4	7.8	13.0	7.1
Total PA-Food-Housing	7.3%	4.8%	8.9%	4.8%	3.6%	15.4%	9.9%	4.6%	−1.7%
Medical Care	3.3%	0.4%	5.1%	8.8%	60.3%	8.4%	11.6%	6.6%	7.1%
Student Assistance					167.0%	19.5%	16.4%	12.9%	−2.5%

Note: Reagan administration figures include four years.

Source: Calculations by author from OMB data.

largest average real growth was observed in the Truman, the second Eisenhower, the Nixon, and the Nixon-Ford administrations. In the 1950s increases in public assistance benefits were coupled with social security increases. In the 1960s they were decoupled. It was during the Nixon administration that public assistance expanded again. The Nixon-Ford increases reveal the effect of the nationalization of Aid to the Blind, Old Age Assistance, and Aid to the Permanently and Totally Disabled into the Supplemental Security Income program. Growth in the Carter years is zero percent despite increases in the low income energy assistance program. Throughout the entire period, growth in public assistance cash programs never achieves the level observed with the other cash programs—retirement and unemployment compensation.

Combining the major cash and in-kind programs for the poor, there are few differences from the pattern of the cash public assistance programs. The food programs show the increases of the latter part of the Eisenhower term and the Johnson and Nixon presidencies. The school milk program was initiated in 1956 and affects the food expenditures during this period. There was some growth resulting from President Kennedy's effort to implement a food stamp program by executive order. A provision of the school lunch program targeted payments toward the poor during this period as well. The real growth began with President Johnson and was greatly expanded by President Nixon. The 56 percent real growth in food and nutrition assistance observed during the Nixon administration is not a latent effect of the Johnson programs. Nixon sought major expansions in the food stamp program. Presidents Carter and Reagan sought to decrease these expenditures. Reagan was quite successful. The housing growth in the Nixon administration does result from the housing acts passed during the Johnson years. Nixon sought to hold down increasing housing costs and issued an administrative freeze in 1973.

With two other programs, the effect of the Johnson administration can be seen. Medical payments and payments to students take off during the Johnson administration. There was a beginning growth in medical payments during the Kennedy administration after years of unsuccessful efforts by Democrats in Congress to enact a health insurance program. The student assistance payments did not really exist before Johnson. There were some higher education assistance loans through universities enacted in 1958, but the education assistance category really begins in 1965.[2]

NEW PROGRAMS FOR INDIVIDUALS

Since 1946, thirty-two new budget accounts have been added for payments to individuals. While this does not mean that these are new programs, it does serve to illustrate where program growth has been and what programs Congress and the president sought to show as separate budget items. Thirteen of these budget accounts are over $1 billion. Seven of the programs are entitlements. The most costly programs were added in the 1960s. The cost of these new, mostly in-kind initiatives is only half of the 1983 cost of the major pre-1947 programs. The big dollars are readily seen in the social insurance entitlement programs for retirement and unemployment. Very little of this money is directly targeted to the poor. During 1983, only $14.6 billion of the $279 billion in pre-1947 programs are low income conditioned. This is less than 5 percent of these dollars. Slightly over a third of the money in large new programs is targeted to the poor. The balance of the money going to the poor is found in small budget accounts.

LOW INCOME PAYMENTS TO INDIVIDUALS

To further understand the bases of these differences within the budget categories, the distinction between cash and in-kind programs and in means tested versus nonmeans tested programs

TABLE 6-6
Payments to Individuals: New Budget Accounts, 1948–1985

Category	Year	Program	Cost	Entitlement	Low Income Program
Employment	1953	Federal Unemployment Benefits			
Insurance	1957	Disability	$18.3		
Food	1958	Special Milk			
Health	1961	Medicaid	19.0	√	Low
Employment	1962	Extended Unemployment Benefits			
Food	1962	Food Stamps	11.8		Low
Employment	1962	Special Workers Compensation Fund			
Other PA	1963	Refugee Assistance			Low
Health	1966	Medicare	38.6	√	
Health	1967	Medicare Supplemental	18.3	√	
Housing	1967	Rural Housing for Domestic Farm Labor			
Education	1968	Student Financial Assistance	4.0		Low
Education	1968	Guaranteed Student Loans	2.6	√	
Insurance	1970	Special Benefits for Disabled Coal Miners	1.1	√	
Housing	1971	Mutual and Self-Help Housing			Low
Food	1972	Section 32 Funds for Strengthening Markets			Low
Other PA	1973	Supplemental Security Income	8.7	√	Low
Food	1976	Special Supplemental Food (WIC)	1.1		Low
Food	1976	Food Donations			Low
Other PA	1976	Earned Income Tax Credit	1.2	√	Low
Employment	1976	Regional Rail Protective Account			
Housing	1976	Low Income Housing Operations	1.5		Low

continued

TABLE 6-6 (*continued*)

Category	Year	Program	Cost	Entitlement	Low Income Program
Social Services	1977	Community Services Administration			Low
Housing	1977	Very Low Income Housing Repair Grants			Low
Veterans	1979	Post-Vietnam Era Veterans Education			
Housing	1979	Troubled Projects Operating Subsidies			Low
Housing	1980	Congregate Housing Program			
Other PA	1981	Low Income Energy Assistance	2.0		Low
Employment	1983	Conrail Labor Assistance			
Food	1983	FEMA Emergency Food Distribution			Low
Food	1983	Nutrition Assistance for Puerto Rico			Low
Housing	1984	Rural Rental Assistance Payments			Low
		Total of large new programs	$128.2		

Note: Year refers to the fiscal year that expenditures occurred, not necessarily the year the program was enacted. Cost is 1983 actual expenditures in billions of current dollars for programs over $1 billion.

Source: Calculation by author from OMB data, 1984.

can be developed further using the data series of OMB payments to individuals for the years 1950–1985. Table 6-8 shows cash and in-kind percent changes with and without veterans dollars. The in-kind changes show a higher rate of increase of the in-kind expenditures during Democratic administrations over Republican administrations. During the Kennedy, Johnson, and Carter administrations, increases for in-kind expenditures are

TABLE 6-7
Payments to Individuals: Large Programs Enacted Before 1946

Category	Enacted	Program	Cost	Entitlement	Low Income Program
Insurance	1935	Social Security	$154.0	✓	
Insurance	1929	Civil Service Retirement	20.8	✓	
Insurance		Military Retirement	15.9	✓	
Insurance	1935	Railroad Retirement	3.8	✓	
Veterans	1929	Compensation	9.8	✓	
Employment	1935	Unemployment Compensation	31.9	✓	
Employment		Advances to Unemployment Fund	11.7	✓	
Health		Health Resources and Services	1.2		
Veterans		VA Medical Care	7.6		
Housing	1937	Subsidized Housing Projects	7.8		
Food	1946	Child Nutrition	3.3	✓	Low
Other PA	1935	Public Assistance (AFDC)	7.9	✓	Low
Veterans	1900	Veterans Nonservice Pensions	3.4	✓	Low
		Total	$279.1		

Note: Cost is 1983 actual expenditures in billions of current dollars for programs over $1 billion.

Source: Calculations by author from OMB data, 1984.

larger than are the increases for cash expenditures. The impact of the Johnson presidency is clearly evident. When Johnson took office, expenditures for in-kind programs constituted only 4 percent of all payments to individuals. When he left office, these payments were 22 percent of all expenditures. This percentage has continued to grow, and by 1985 in-kind expenditures were one third of all payments to individuals. This growth has been influenced predominately by food and health expenditures.

The in-kind expenditures comprise a much larger proportion of controllable expenditures than do the cash expenditures. Food and housing expenditures are classified as controllable throughout most of the series. These are the expenditures that have increased more under Democratic administrations. Payments to individuals do not include many education, social service, and manpower programs that were also initiated in the Kennedy and Johnson years.

The means tested versus nonmeans tested cash benefits comparison shows differences between Republican and Democratic positions. First, the figures in Table 6-8 indicate that cash benefits were increased the most in the Truman and Eisenhower administrations. This reflects the first efforts to adjust social security and the public assistance benefit programs. The former is nonmeans tested; the latter are means tested. The next period of growth is during the Nixon administration. Growth in the cash programs is generally smaller during the Democratic administrations. The lowest growth period in real terms is during the Reagan administration.

The increases in the cash programs for public assistance are much lower than are nonmeans cash benefit increases. The only period which shows high levels of growth in low income cash programs is during the Nixon and Ford administrations. Before this time, the disparity between growth in means and nonmeans cash benefits was the largest during the Republican administrations rather than the Democratic administrations. Real growth in means tested cash programs came to an abrupt halt with the Ford administration and then declines for the rest of the period.

TABLE 6-8

Average Real Changes in Payments to Individuals by Presidential Administrations,
for Cash and In-kind Benefits, 1950–1985

	Truman	Eisenhower I	Eisenhower II	Kennedy	Johnson	Nixon	Nixon–Ford	Carter	Reagan*
Cash	9.5%	12.3%	13.0%	3.3%	6.0%	10.7%	7.9%	3.2%	1.5%
In-kind	−10.7	0.6	−0.2	1.9	47.3	15.0	10.2	6.4	4.3
Total	1.8%	10.0%	11.3%	3.2%	11.0%	11.8%	8.5%	4.1%	2.4%

* Reagan administration changes based on four-year averages using estimated outlays for FY84 and FY85.

Note: All percentages are change in actual outlays for the current fiscal year over actual outlays for the previous fiscal averaged over presidential administrations in real 1972 dollars.

Source: Calculations by author from OMB data, 1984.

Average Real Changes in Payments to Individuals by Presidential Administration for Cash and In-kind
Benefits without Veterans' Benefits, 1950–1985

	Truman	Eisenhower I	Eisenhower II	Kennedy	Johnson	Nixon	Nixon–Ford	Carter	Reagan*
Cash	12.8%	15.3%	14.9%	3.6%	6.6%	11.6%	8.5%	3.4%	1.6%
In-kind	6.9	9.5	14.5	15.1	84.6	15.1	11.9	8.2	4.8
Total	12.6%	15.1%	14.9%	4.0%	12.4%	12.4%	9.4%	4.8%	2.6%

* Reagan administration changes based on four-year averages using estimated outlays for FY84 and FY85.

Note: All percentages are change in actual outlays for the current fiscal year over actual outlays for the previous fiscal averaged over presidential administrations in real 1972 dollars.

Source: Calculations by author from OMB data, 1984.

TABLE 6-9
Average Real Changes in Payments to Individuals by Presidential Administration for Low Income Benefits without Veterans' Benefits, 1950–1985

	Truman	Eisenhower I	Eisenhower II	Kennedy	Johnson	Nixon	Nixon–Ford	Carter	Reagan*
Cash	6.9%	2.5%	6.5%	5.4%	3.8%	9.6%	11.9%	1.9%	-3.8%
In-kind	5.9	13.1	19.0	16.0	71.0	26.2	12.5	7.0	0.8
AFDC	6.9	2.5	6.5	5.4	3.8	9.4	-5.3	-1.0	-8.7
Total	7.0%	3.4%	7.9%	7.3%	35.3%	18.9%	12.3%	5.2%	-0.3%

*Reagan administration changes based on four-year averages using estimated outlays for FY84 and FY85.

Note: All percentages are change in actual outlays for the current fiscal year over actual outlays for the previous fiscal averaged over presidential administrations in real 1972 dollars.

Source: Calculations by author from OMB data.

The AFDC series shows this effect even more starkly. Throughout the entire series the low growth in the cash public assistance programs shows the preference for insurance programs and the reliance on in-kind assistance for the poor.

It is in the in-kind low income benefits that the Democratic presidents generally show higher levels of increases. Growth in in-kind benefits exceeds that of cash benefits in the Kennedy, Johnson, and Carter presidencies. Reagan was not able to decrease the growth rate of in-kind benefits to the same extent that cash benefits were slowed.

The impact and priorities of the Democratic administrations were also seen earlier in the education, manpower, and social services category of the budget. The Democratic presidents were the most active and the most successful. The Truman, Kennedy, and Johnson requests were the highest; the Republican requests were the lowest. It is in this category that the break between the Johnson and Nixon presidencies is the most evident. The social service programs were the ones which Nixon sought to end. President Nixon expanded many programs, but fought the programs created under the OEO umbrella. Johnson had his greatest effect by immediately increasing expenditures in this category. President Kennedy was also active and successful in securing enactment of the Manpower and Training Act of 1962 and the Public Assistance Amendments of 1962 which authorized payments for social services. The increases in the late Eisenhower years were the result of Sputnik response. Growth moderated in the Ford and Carter administrations despite the growth in manpower and public service jobs during this time. This category is also the one that Reagan had the most effect in cutting.

At the beginning of this series, cash payments were 90 percent of all low income benefits to individuals. In 1962 they were 81 percent. Eight years later after the Johnson administration, low income cash benefits were less than half of all payments to the poor. The downward trend continued steadily to 26 percent in 1985. The provisions for food, housing, and health care far exceed cash payments to the poor. Their growth is influenced by the cost of these items and by demand. That is, it is determined to a large extent by the number of eligible individuals. Cash payments for the poor require legislative action to increase benefits.

PRESIDENTIAL REQUESTS AND CONGRESSIONAL DIVERGENCE

Despite presidential interest, Congress has not always followed the recommendations of Democratic presidents to increase cash programs. The Truman, Johnson, and Carter recommendations for cash expenditures have been higher than what actually resulted. The increases which Democratic presidents have sought for low income programs have not always occurred either. Carter's negative proposals reflect, in part, efforts to decrease food programs in the face of rising unemployment and food costs which forced expenditures higher.

At the same time Congress has resisted the efforts of Republican presidents to decrease spending for low income programs. Once again the efforts of the Nixon administration to increase low income programs stands out as does the Reagan administration's efforts to decrease them. The second Eisenhower administration, the Ford administration, and the Carter administration recommended decreases. Only the Reagan administration was successful in achieving decreases. Overall, Democrats received less and Republicans generally received more than they asked for. The budget outlays under new legislative authority also show these intentions.

ESTIMATION OF POLITICAL AND ECONOMIC INFLUENCES

We have to this point been describing changes in spending on an average basis across administrations. These relationships can

TABLE 6-10
Real Changes in Average Presidential Requests and Actual
Expenditures for Cash and Low Income Programs, 1950–1984

	All Cash		All Low Income	
	Request	Actual	Request	Actual
Truman	15.6%	8.3%	10.1%	7.3%
Eisenhower I	5.4	12.4	10.6	4.3
Eisenhower II	1.3	13.4	−0.3	8.4
Kennedy	3.6	3.2	10.8	5.7
Johnson	14.7	4.6	8.8	5.3
Nixon	5.9	11.4	19.3	20.1
Nixon–Ford	2.3	7.5	−0.7	11.7
Carter	1.5	3.4	−1.0	7.0
Reagan*	1.4	5.4	−7.9	1.2

*Reagan requests based on three years; actual on first two years.

Note: Requests are the percentage change in appropriations requested in the president's current budget over actual outlays for the previous fiscal year. Actual indicates the percentage change in actual outlays for the current fiscal year over actual outlays for the previous fiscal year. All are averages over presidential administrations in real 1972 dollars.

Source: Calculations by author from executive budget data.

be seen more precisely through statistical estimations. Coefficients of the effect which presidents, Congress, and economic conditions have on social spending can be estimated through time series regression using changes in spending in the general categories we have been describing. This permits the analysis of the effect of presidents while at the same time considering the effect of the Congress, economic conditions, and the political calendar.

All of the data are measured in real terms as percent changes over the previous fiscal year. Changes in expenditures are modeled as a function of the change in the level of unemployment, the number of House nonsouthern Democrats, and the presidential administration. Alternative methods of assessing the

TABLE 6-11
New Recommended Outlays for Cash and Low Income
Programs, 1950–1985*
(in millions of real dollars)

	Cash	Low Income
Truman	$1,411.1	$674.8
Eisenhower I	589.4	451.6
Eisenhower II	147.1	0
Kennedy	1,493.6	1,048.2
Johnson	8,116.6	377.5
Nixon	9,610.4	975.8
Nixon–Ford	−4,609.1	−1,700.5
Carter	550.9	999.1
Reagan*	−6,136.8	−4,266.7

*Includes food, housing, and public assistance without veterans benefits.

Note: Figures are the sum of all new recommended outlays in each administration. Reagan administration includes recommendations for all four years.

Source: Calculations by author from executive budget data.

presidential effect are also explored. The estimates in Table 6-12 use a dummy variable for each presidential administration. Using these variables it is hypothesized that each president will have a different effect on social spending. The congressional variable is included to test the hypothesis that changes in social spending will be larger when the number of House nonsouthern Democrats elected to the House of Representatives increases. The unemployment change variable measures the difference in the level of unemployment from fiscal year to fiscal year. For example, if unemployment increased from 5 percent to 7 percent this change is measured as 2 percent. A decline in unemployment would have a negative sign.

These estimates confirm the relationships we have been describing using the average changes within administrations. To see the effect of an individual administration, the coefficients

TABLE 6-12
Estimation of Real Percent Changes in All Federal Expenditures,
Social Welfare Expenditures and Nonsocial Welfare Expenditures,
1950–1985

	All Expenditures	Social Welfare Expenditures	Nonsocial Welfare Expenditures
House nonsouthern Democrats	−0.06% (0.1)	0.11% (0.08)	−0.11% (0.12)
Unemployment $(\%_t - \%_{t-1})$	0.4 (1.4)	6.0** (1.2)	−2.0 (1.7)
Constant	23.3 (12.8)	−9.4 (11.0)	33.9* (15.9)
Eisenhower I	−18.6** (5.7)	5.9 (4.9)	−25.4** (7.1)
Eisenhower II	−11.1 (5.9)	2.1 (5.1)	−15.6* (7.3)
Kennedy	−11.4 (5.7)	0.01 (4.9)	−15.7* (7.1)
Johnson	−5.2 (6.9)	5.4 (6.0)	−9.8 (8.6)
Nixon	−11.6 (6.3)	1.4 (5.5)	−18.9* (7.9)
Nixon–Ford	−9.1 (7.4)	−4.4 (6.4)	−13.2 (9.2)
Carter	−8.4 (8.5)	−7.0 (7.3)	−9.0 (10.5)
Reagan I	−10.1 (6.8)	−7.5 (5.9)	−9.4 (8.4)
$\bar{Y}$	5.2%	7.0%	4.3%
N	36	36	36
R^2	0.58	0.62	0.45
Durbin-Watson statistic	2.5	2.3	2.4

*Significant at 0.05 level.
**Significant at 0.01 level.

Note: Number in parentheses are standard errors. Presidential variables are dummy variables coded as +1 for each four year term. Reagan administration figures include four years.

must be compared with each other. The effect of the Truman administration is included in the constant term. The size of the individual coefficients are in the same order as the ranking of administrations observed earlier for total budget growth. Growth is generally higher during Republican administrations.

Each of the presidential coefficients controls for the effect of the other variables in the equation. This means that the effect of an individual administration on budget outlays is the effect while considering the number of House nonsouthern Democrats and the level of unemployment. This allows us to isolate the effect of the presidential administration from the other policy influences we are considering.

The social welfare budget estimates show a strong relationship with unemployment. A 1 percent change in unemployment results in a 6 percent increase in all federal social welfare expenditures. The negative coefficients obtained after adding the presidential effect to the constant is countered by the positive effect of the size of the Democratic margin in Congress. This suggests that the size of the nonsouthern Democratic margin in Congress has an effect which interacts in some way with presidency variable.

The estimation of all nonsocial welfare expenditures also indicates the divergence between social welfare and other spending. For example, the Eisenhower and Nixon administrations show a greater negative effect with other spending than with social welfare spending. Unemployment has little effect on other expenditures, while it exerts a strong effect on social welfare expenditures.

The relationships with social welfare expenditures are seen in Table 6-13, in which estimates of real changes in total, cash, and in-kind payments to individuals without any veterans expenditures are shown. Expenditures increased at the largest rate in the Truman, Eisenhower, Johnson, and Nixon administrations. They are lowest in the Kennedy, Nixon-Ford, Carter, and Reagan administrations. They increase 5.4 percent with each 1 percent change in unemployment. In-kind expenditures are not related

TABLE 6-13
Estimation of Real Percent Changes in Total, Cash, and In-Kind
Social Welfare Expenditures with Presidential Variables

	All Social Welfare	Cash Social Welfare	In-kind Social Welfare
House nonsouthern Democrats	0.014% (0.06)	−0.014% (0.06)	0.64% (0.38)
Unemployment $(\%_t - \%_{t-1})$	5.4** (0.8)	5.5** (0.8)	5.0 (5.1)
Constant	13.2 (7.8)	16.8 (7.7)	−69.6 (48.2)
Eisenhower I	−1.1 (3.5)	−1.8 (3.5)	11.6 (21.6)
Eisenhower II	−3.2 (3.6)	−3.2 (3.5)	−6.5 (22.1)
Kennedy	−9.1* (3.5)	−9.2* (3.4)	−3.4 (21.4)
Johnson	−1.2 (4.2)	−6.0 (4.2)	50.2 (26.0)
Nixon	−5.3 (3.8)	−5.9 (3.8)	−13.6 (23.9)
Nixon–Ford	−9.2 (4.5)	−9.2* (4.4)	−28.2 (27.8)
Carter	−10.6* (5.2)	−10.4* (5.1)	−40.8 (31.9)
Reagan I	−13.5** (4.1)	−13.7** (4.1)	−29.1 (25.6)
$\bar{Y}$	9.8%	8.7%	19.0%
N	36	36	36
R^2	0.76	0.79	0.52
Durbin-Watson statistic	2.2	2.4	2.4

*Significant at 0.05 level.
**Significant at 0.01 level.

Note: Numbers in parentheses are standard errors. Presidential variables are dummy variables coded as +1 for each four year term. Figures exclude veterans expenditures. Reagan administration figures include four years.

to unemployment as are cash expenditures. In-kind expenditures are higher than cash expenditures in the Kennedy administration, but lower than cash in the Truman and Carter administrations. The Johnson administration shows the highest rate of growth in in-kind expenditures.

The models to explain social spending can be simplified by including the information about the patterns of spending under the different administrations in several summary variables. These variables include the unemployment and the number of House nonsouthern Democrats variable as before. A dummy variable is coded as 1 for Democratic presidents and 0 for Republican presidents. Another variable is included to capture an interactive effect between the size of the nonsouthern Democratic margin in the House and the party of the president. It is hypothesized that the size of this margin affects Democratic presidents differently than it affects Republican presidents.[3]

In the patterns of growth of in-kind expenditures and in the statistical estimations, the Carter administration stands apart from the other Democratic administrations. Alternative codings for these years were evaluated. In the estimations in Table 6–14 for in-kind expenditures, the Carter administration is coded as a Republican administration.[4]

Coefficients were obtained by using the OMB series of payments to individuals broken into cash and in-kind components. A percent change in unemployment results in a 5 percent increase in social spending. Controlling for other variables spending is 6.5 percent higher under Republican presidents than under Democratic presidents. The coefficient of House nonsouthern Democrats is negative, indicating that the percent change in social welfare expenditures was higher during periods in which there were fewer nonsouthern Democrats in the House of Representatives.

The estimations with cash and in-kind payments to individuals highlight differences in the patterns of spending that we have been observing throughout this discussion. As with total expenditures, the negative presidential party coefficient is not

TABLE 6-14
Estimation of Real Percent Changes in Total, Cash, and In-kind
Social Welfare Expenditures with Interaction Variable

	All Social Welfare	Cash Social Welfare	In-kind[1] Social Welfare
House Nonsouthern	−0.11*	−0.13**	−0.032
Democrats	(0.05)	(0.05)	(0.17)
Unemployment	5.0**	5.2**	2.62
$(\%_t-\%_{t-1})$	(1.0)	(0.9)	(4.0)
President[2]	−6.5	−2.0	−251.1**
	(11.0)	(10.3)	(52.1)
Interaction[3]	0.056	0.02	1.9**
	(0.07)	(0.07)	(0.35)
Constant	25.1**	26.9**	14.6
	(7.1)	(6.6)	(26.1)
$\bar{Y}$	9.8%	8.7%	19.0%
N	36	36	36
R^2	0.57	0.65	0.55
Durbin-Watson statistic	1.67	1.93	2.02

*Significant at 0.05 level.
**Significant at 0.01 level.
[1] Carter is coded as a Republican administration.
[2] Presidential variable is a dummy variable coded as +1 for Democrats and 0 for Republicans.
[3] The interaction term is the number of House nonsouthern Democrats times the party of the president. Thus, it is zero during Republican administrations.

Note: Numbers in parentheses are standard errors. Figures exclude veterans expenditures.

statistically significant in the cash equation. Cash expenditures increase with unemployment and have increased more during periods when there have been fewer nonsouthern Democrats in Congress. The net effect is that cash payments to individuals have increased more during Republican administrations than during Democratic administrations.

In-kind expenditures follow a different dynamic. First, they do not show the effect of unemployment. Second, the effect of the number of House nonsouthern Democrats differs during Democratic and Republican presidencies. Third, there is a major change in the presidential party relationship following the first Nixon presidency. The Carter administration does not show the same effect on in-kind expenditures as do the previous Democratic administrations.

During the Republican and all post-Nixon administrations, the following effects are observed: expenditure changes are predicted to be equal to 14.6 − 0.03 percent times the number of House nonsouthern Democrats (from 100 to 180). This results in changes between 9 and 12 percent. During Democratic presidencies, the size of the House nonsouthern Democratic margin serves to increase the change in in-kind expenditures by 1.9 percent per each additional member. The net effect is a positive 1.87 percent times the number of House nonsouthern Democrats minus 251 percent plus 14.6 percent. During the Johnson administration with 184 House nonsouthern Democrats, the increase would be predicted as 108 percent. During the Kennedy administration with only 140 nonsouthern members of the House, expenditures are predicted to be increased 25 percent. The first Nixon administration is a transition between the Johnson presidency and the second Nixon administration.

The size of this House margin is what distinguishes the Kennedy, Johnson, and Nixon increases of in-kind expenditures. This effect is seen in the initiation tables where both the Congress and the president were creating new in-kind programs during the Johnson and Nixon administrations. This stimulative effect ended after Nixon and is not observed during the subsequent Democratic presidency of Jimmy Carter. A similar effect is seen with income tested in-kind programs. The Ford, Carter, and Reagan presidencies all tried to achieve savings in the food and health care programs.

A similar pattern of results is observed with low income benefits. These cash benefits do not show the inverse relationship with House nonsouthern Democrats. The in-kind benefits fol-

TABLE 6-15

Estimation of Real Percent Changes in Total, Cash, and In-kind Low Income Social Welfare Expenditures with Interaction Variable

	All Low Income	Cash Social Welfare	In-kind[1] Social Welfare
House Nonsouthern Democrats	0.04 (0.07)	0.007 (0.07)	−0.11 (0.09)
Unemployment $(\%_t - \%_{t-1})$	4.2** (1.5)	4.4** (1.4)	3.9** (2.0)
President[2]	10.3 (17.3)	21.3 (15.9)	−114.5** (26.9)
Interaction[3]	−0.047 (0.1)	−0.12 (0.1)	0.88** (0.18)
Constant	0.8 (11.1)	2.5 (10.2)	28.9* (13.5)
$\bar{Y}$	8.7%	5.0%	16.2%
N	36	36	36
R^2	0.20	0.29	0.52
Durbin-Watson statistic	1.36	2.01	1.89

*Significant at 0.05 level.

**Significant at 0.01 level.

[1]Carter is coded as a Republican administration.

[2]Presidential variable is a dummy variable coded as +1 for Democrats and 0 for Republicans.

[3]The interaction term is the number of House nonsouthern Democrats times the party of the president. Thus, it is zero during Republican administrations.

Note: Numbers in parentheses are standard errors. Figures exclude veterans expenditures.

low the same pattern of growth as all in-kind benefits with two notable exceptions. First, the size of the increases is smaller. Second, the increases are related to levels of unemployment, whereas all in-kind benefits were not.

None of the estimations show any election cycle or honeymoon effects. Expenditures were not larger during election years on a two-year or a four-year cycle. There was no evidence of any cycle indicating that expenditures increased more early in presidential administrations. Earlier research had found evidence of an election cycle only with average benefits for social security and not with any other benefit series. Some of the cyclical regularity observed previously may be due to cycles in unemployment or numbers of Democrats in Congress.

EXPLAINING PRESIDENTIAL AND CONGRESSIONAL RELATIONSHIPS

The cyclical pattern of unemployment has been observed before. Unemployment tends to increase during Republican administrations and decline during Democratic administrations. The Carter administration was an exception. Unemployment began to increase during the latter part of this Democratic administration. Consequently, unemployment peaked midway through the subsequent Republican administration and was declining during the latter part of Reagan's first term. This cyclical pattern of unemployment affects social spending.

The negative relationship of House nonsouthern Democrats and social spending is also due in part to the effect of economic conditions on numbers of Democrats elected to the House. These new members take office after the recessions have peaked and unemployment is declining. Their increased numbers in Congress are usually associated with declining expenditures for social programs associated with declining unemployment.

The major expansions of the social insurance programs have also occurred during Republican administrations. These programs are responsive to unemployment changes as well because eligible persons often choose to retire if they lose their job in a recession. In-kind programs are much less responsive to unemployment than are the cash programs.

More new programs have been enacted during Democratic than during Republican administrations. In the in-kind area these enactments show up as increased expenditures with a shorter lag period. Most of the program initiations occurred during the Kennedy and Johnson administrations. What distinguishes these two administrations is the size of the House nonsouthern Democratic majority. Congressional leadership changes much less often than does presidential leadership. Congress has been considering and often rejecting new programs for some time before they are ultimately enacted. For a Democratic president to succeed with a proposal for a new program, sufficient numbers of new nonsouthern Democrats in Congress were required to overcome committee leadership resistance.

The lower change figures under Democratic administrations are not due to lack of presidential interest. Democrats generally ask for more and get less of what they ask. The requests of Republican presidents are usually bid up by the Democratic congresses. This dynamic is also seen with the benefit adjustments for social programs.

7

Benefit Adjustments

Of the reasons cited previously for the growth of social welfare expenditures, benefit adjustments are the most visible and direct means of increasing expenditures. Closely related are changes in eligibility conditions. The latter also have a direct effect, but the way these adjustments affect expenditures is usually less visible and often times less fully comprehended. Today almost all federal social welfare programs have benefits and eligibility indexed automatically for price changes. This is a very recent phenomenon. From 1950 to 1968, benefit adjustments were made in an *ad hoc* fashion by political leaders. Political and economic conditions triggered these adjustments. From 1969 to 1980 the Congress had a case of indexing fever. During the first Reagan presidency, as the cost of these provisions began to mount, indexed provisions were modified.

The patterns and causes of benefit adjustments can be seen by examining these three time periods: pre-1969, post-1969, and post-1981. The pre- and post-1969 periods are seen distinctly in Table 7-1. The cash programs in Table 7-2 do not look any different. The major federal income security programs—social security, public assistance, veterans benefits, and food stamps—are examined in more detail. From this analysis, the interaction of politics and economics is seen in decisions to adjust certain social programs.

TABLE 7-1
Social Program Indexing by Periods

	Income Security	Public Assistance	Food	Housing	Social Services	Employment	Manpower	Health	Education	Veterans	Total
1950–1960									1		1
1961–1964	2										2
1965–1968	1			1				1	1		4
1969–1972	5		2		1	1	1	1			11
1973–1976	2	1	7	3	4	1	1	3	4		26
1977–1980		1	1	1	1		8		4	1	17
Total	10	2	10	5	6	2	10	5	10	1	61

Source: Calculations by author from *Indexation of Federal Programs*, prepared by the Congressional Research Service for the Committee on the Budget, U.S. Senate (May 1981).

TABLE 7-2
Indexed Cash Programs

	Income Security	Employment	Public Assistance	Total
1950–1960				
1961–1964	3			3
1965–1968				
1969–1972	5	1		6
1973–1976	1	1	1	3
1977–1980			1	1
Total	9	2	2	13

Source: Calculations by author from *Indexation of Federal Programs*, 1981.

AD HOC BENEFIT ADJUSTMENTS, 1946–1969

Prior to 1969 there were only seven indexed programs. Three of these were benefit programs for federal workers; the other four programs were implicitly indexed. This means that federal expenditures rose automatically with factors outside of the federal government's control. For example, expenditures for two education programs grew with local expenditures for education. Medicare expenditures were implicitly linked to health care costs. Expenditures for one housing program grew with the cost of housing. The early indexing of these four programs is due to the nature of these expenditures; the decisions on the three federal benefit programs reflect their jurisdiction by the Post Office and Civil Service Committee rather than the Ways and Means Committee which had jurisdiction over the other cash benefit programs during this period. The benefit adjustments of these other cash programs, while occurring in an *ad hoc* fashion, were triggered by the underlying political and economic conditions. These conditions and their results can be seen in the following examination of the social security, public assistance, and veterans', benefit programs.

SOCIAL SECURITY

The Social Security Act of 1935 established Old Age Insurance as a retirement insurance program in which eligibility and benefits were "earned" through employment in which both the employee and employer pay a tax into a trust fund.[1] From 1935 to 1950 few changes were made to the act.[2] The 1939 amendments were the first and only major amendments to the Social Security Act during this period. These changes advanced the first payment of benefits from 1942 to 1940. They also permitted survivors and dependents to be eligible for benefits and modified the eligibility requirements for benefits. President Truman requested increases in social security benefits in messages to Congress in 1947, 1948, 1949, and 1950. These increases were passed in the House in 1949 and by the Senate in 1950. They were far-reaching reforms that increased benefits an average of 77 percent, extended coverage to 9.2 million persons, increased the wage base and tax schedule, eased eligibility for benefits, and increased the amount of earnings permitted by retirees without loss of benefits. Congress did not enact the disability or health insurance requested by the president.

Over the next thirty years social security evolved through similar modifications and extensions.[3] Some of these were the result of presidential initiatives; others originated in Congress. The advisory commissions established by statute in 1956 were important in moving social security issues onto the agenda during this period.[4] Economic conditions influenced social security reform by creating conditions for benefit increases and by making the financing of the increases possible.[5] Political conditions expedited and incremented the proposed benefit increases.

The enactment of general benefit increases for social security are detailed in Table 7-3. Benefits were increased 10 times by congressional action from 1947 to 1977 and three times by automatic increases. One increase (1970) died when the House had insufficient time for a conference agreement; another increase

TABLE 7-3
Social Security Initiatives, 1947–1977

Year	President	Presidential Recommendation	Congressional Action
1947	Truman	increase	none
1948	Truman	50% increase	none
1949	Truman	50% increase	H: 70–100% increase
1950	Truman	50% increase	S: 70–100% increase
1952	Truman	12.5%	12.5% increase enacted
1954	Eisenhower	increase	13% increase enacted
1958	Eisenhower	no request	7% increase enacted[a]
1961	Kennedy	minimun benefit	enacted increase[b]
1965	Johnson	7% increase	7% increase enacted
1967	Johnson	15% increase	H: 12.5%; S: 15%; 13% enacted
1969	Nixon	10%	S: 15%; H: 15%; 15% enacted
1970	Nixon	no request	H: 5%; S: 10%; Died
1971	Nixon	6% increase	S: 10%; H: 10%; enacted
1972	Nixon	no request	S: 20%; H: 20%; enacted
1973	Nixon		S: 5.9%; enacted
1974	Nixon		H: 11%; enacted
1975	Ford	5% limit	8%[c]
1976	Ford		6.4%
1977	Carter		5.9%
1978	Carter		6.5%
1979	Carter		9.9%
1980	Carter		14.3%
1981	Reagan		11.2%
1982	Reagan		7.4%
1983	Reagan		3.5%

Key: H = House; S = Senate.
[a]Initiated in House.
[b]No general benefit increase requested or enacted; minimum benefit refers to lowest benefit payable.
[c]All increases from 1975 on are automatic per legislation enacted in 1972 and amended in 1974. Ford sought to limit the automatic increase to 5 percent in 1976.

Source: Calculations by author from *Social Security Bulletins.*

was set aside when Congress enacted an even larger increase in the same year. A few general observations can be made about the increases detailed in Table 7-3. All benefits requested by the president were enacted. After 1969 it was the Senate which took the initiative in legislating benefit increases. Benefit increases were much more frequent after 1969 than before; rapid increases in prices after 1969 contributed to these increases.

TABLE 7-4
Relationship of Consumer Price and Social Security Benefits,
1949–1980

Date Enacted	Date Effective	Statutory Increase	Effective Increase	CPI Change	Cumulative Benefit Change	Cumulative CPI Change
8-50	9-50[a]	77.0%	81.3%	75.5%	77.0%	75.5%
7-52	9-52	12.5	14.1	9.3	99.1	91.8
9-54	9-54	13.0	13.3	0.5	125.0	92.8
8-58	1-59	7.0	7.7	8.0	140.8	108.2
7-65	1-65[b]	7.0	7.7	7.9	157.7	124.7
12-67	2-68	13.0	14.2	9.2	191.2	145.4
12-69	1-70	15.0	15.6	10.8	234.9	171.9
3-71[c]	1-71	10.0	10.4	5.2	268.4	186.0
7-72	9-72	20.0	20.7	5.9	342.1	202.9
6-73[d]	6-74	5.9				
12-73	3-74	7.0				
	6-74	4.0		16.4	390.7	252.6
	6-75[e]	8.0		9.3	430.0	285.4
	6-76	6.4		5.9	463.9	308.1
	6-77	5.9		6.9	497.2	336.3
	6-78	6.5		7.4	536.0	368.6
	6-79	9.9		11.1	599.0	420.6
	6-80	14.3		14.2	699.0	494.2

[a]Increase effective 9-50 for current retires; increase effective 4-52 for future retires.
[b]Increase retroactive to 1-65.
[c]Increase retroactive.
[d]Superceded by 11% increase enacted in 12-73.
[e]After 1975 all increases are automatic.

Source: *Indexation of Federal Programs,* 1981, p. 165.

The relationship between benefit increases and consumer prices shown in Table 7-4 indicates the extent to which social security benefits have kept pace with prices. Excluding the automatic increases, seven of ten increases have exceeded the increases in consumer prices from the date of the last benefit increase. The largest increases over inflation occur in Republican administrations under Eisenhower in 1954 and Nixon in 1969 and 1971.

A political factor which has expedited these increases has been the cost of living adjustments recommended by newly elected presidents in their first year in office. The figures in Table 7-5 indicate that first term presidents generally recommend increases just enough to match inflation and, many times, less than the price changes. Both Eisenhower and Kennedy made social security recommendations during their first year in office but made no recommendations for benefit increases because changes in the price level were very small since the last legislative increase. There was no effort to raise the absolute level of social security benefits by the presidents in their first terms.

TABLE 7-5
First Term Presidential Social Security Increases

Year	President	Presidential Request[a]	CPI Change[b]	Actual Enactment[c]
1949–50	Truman	50%	75.5%	77%
1953	Eisenhower	0	1.0	0
1961	Kennedy	0	2.6	0
1965	Johnson	7	7.9	7
1969	Nixon	10	10.8	15
1975	Ford	5	9.3	8

[a]Recommendations by presidents for general Social Security benefit increases in the first year of presidential terms.
[b]Consumer price index change since previous benefit increase.
[c]Actual benefit increase enacted.

Source: Presidential messages and annual *Social Security Bulletins.*

While the newly elected presidents have recommended benefit increases, the composition and party of Congress have been
important in determining the size of the increase actually enacted. In 1949–1950, 1969, and 1975 when Congress was controlled by Democrats, the legislated increases exceeded the
presidential request. Benefit increases in 1971 and 1972 were
also enacted by Democratic congresses and exceeded the
amount of increase supported by the president.

Incumbent presidents have also made midterm social security recommendations. Of the six benefit increases not occurring at the onset of presidential terms, three were recommended
by incumbent presidents who were eligible for another elected
term. These were recommended by Truman in 1952, Eisenhower in 1954, and Johnson in 1967. All of these proposed increases exceeded the price increases from the date of the last
benefit increase. The 1958 increase, although enacted just prior
to the midterm election, simply matched the cost of living increase. In this case, Eisenhower indicated that the cost of living
adjustment was acceptable.[6]

Accounts of social security policy describe a proclivity for
election year benefit increases during the 1950s and increases
prompted by a concern for high inflation in the 1970s. Derthick
observes "that election year action became the pattern in the
1950s, but Congress kept its options open and in the 1960s acted
irregularly in response to particular combinations of political
and economic pressures and opportunities."[7]

In sum, social security benefits have been influenced by a
combination of political and economic factors. Presidents of
both parties have supported adjustments to keep pace with inflation at the onset of their terms. The Democratic Congress has
been responsible for increasing these adjustments beyond that
required to match price increases. Presidential support for benefit increases differs when a presidential election is imminent. In
the 1970s there was an increase in legislative activity on benefit
increases during a period of rapid inflation, Democratic congresses, and Republican presidents. In contrast to previous in-

creases, the initiative for these later increases arose in the Senate. Benefit increases were made automatic, effective in 1975, triggered by cost of living increases over the previous year.

The analysis here suggests that price increases and newly elected presidents are conditions for maintenance of the buying power of social security dollars. Beyond this the Congress plays an important role. This analysis also suggests the inadequacy of Tufte's presidential dominated election cycle thesis.[8] Social security policy has been an area of active bipartisan presidential and congressional interest. This degree of interest and support does not extend to other programs.

PUBLIC ASSISTANCE

The pattern of benefit increases observed with the public assistance programs indicates a greater degree of independence and divergence from presidential interests.[9] From 1948 to 1977 public assistance benefits were increased eight times; only two of these increases were requested by presidents. Of the eight increases enacted, five were initiated within the Senate. There were also three other Senate initiated increases that were not enacted.

This absence of presidential initiative in benefit increases does not signify a lack of presidential interest in public assistance or welfare reform. Every president has proposed legislation to restructure or modify the benefits. President Eisenhower encountered opposition to most of his proposals. His proposals to reduce federal public assistance participation were routinely ignored. A variable benefit rate based on state per capita income which he proposed in 1954 was enacted in 1958. President Kennedy's requested welfare amendments were enacted in 1962.[10]

A number of changes in public assistance occurred in the 1960s. Prior to 1967, the Aid to the Blind, the Old Age Assistance, and the Aid to Families with Dependent Children programs were all adjusted at the same time. In the late 1960s, with the AFDC cost rapidly increasing, the House Ways and Means Committee began to take an active interest in the AFDC program's work requirements and supported a freeze on total AFDC expenditures.

While President Nixon's effort to reform AFDC through the enactment of a form of guaranteed income failed, Congress in 1972 did restructure the programs aiding the "deserving poor"— Aid to the Blind, Old Age Assistance, and Aid to the Permanently and Totally Disabled, into the federal Supplemental Security Income program.[11] Under these amendments the federal government sets minimum benefit levels and eligibility conditions.

The benefit formula for public assistance programs is a

TABLE 7-6
Changes in Public Assistance Benefits and the Consumer Price Index,
1947–1965[a]

Year	Quarter	AFDC[a]	Percent Change[b]	Aid to the Blind[a]	Percent Change[b]	CPI[c]	Percent Change
1947	1	$63.34		$37.60		64.80	
1948	4	71.88	13.5%	43.55	15.8%	72.60	12.0%
1950	4	71.44[d]	−0.6	46.00	5.6	74.10	2.1
1951	1	75.01	4.4	46.69	7.2	76.80	5.8[e]3.6[f]
1952	4	82.08	14.9[f]	53.50	14.6[g]	80.10	4.3[g](8.1)[f]
1956	4	95.03	15.8	63.12	18.0	82.60	3.1
1958	4	106.60	12.2	68.30	8.2	86.70	5.0
1965	4	148.10	38.9	93.15	36.4	95.10	9.7

[a]The AFDC and Aid to the Blind dollar amounts are average monthly benefits.

[b]The percentages are changes since the last benefit increase.

[c]Consumer price index 1967 = 100.

[d]The AFDC benefit increase was effective December 1950, while the Aid to the Blind increase was effective in 1951 first quarter.

[e]Calculated from 1948 first quarter for comparison with the AFDC increase.

[f]Calculated from 1950 fourth quarter for comparison with AFDC increase.

[g]Calculated from 1951 first quarter for comparison with Aid to the Blind increase.

matching formula in which the federal government pays a portion of the benefits per individual.[12] Benefit increases have occurred through increases in the federal matching contribution. State responses to the changes in benefit formula will vary. Some states may be spending considerably below the maximum; others spend considerably above. The net effect of the federal formula changes should be to raise benefits for individuals and be reflected in the average benefit.

There are two ways to compare the public assistance benefit increase to the increases in the price index. One way is to compute the percent change in benefits of a state that was always spending just the maximum the federal government was matching. The second way is to compute the percent change in benefits actually paid to individuals after a legislative change. The data in Table 7-6 show the changes in average benefits and their relationship to changes in the consumer price index. After 1950 all of the increases exceeded the price increases since the last benefit adjustment.

FOOD STAMPS

The food stamp program has a shorter history and has undergone fewer changes. It was implemented as a pilot program in 1961 under executive authority. The first program was authorized in 1964 and extended in 1970, 1973, and 1977. The 1970 changes authorized the secretary of agriculture to set uniform national standards for participation and to set a coupon allotment at a level to provide a "nutritionally adequate diet." The secretary was also authorized to make annual adjustments in the cost of coupons to reflect increases in the cost of living index for food. Legislation in 1973 mandated expansion to all areas of the country.

Although case studies credit individual members of Congress with relentless efforts to enact a food stamp program, the recommendations of presidents in their first term shaped the program

TABLE 7-7
Public Assistance Initiatives, 1947–1967

Year	Initiative	Action
1948	Senate	Passed over presidential veto
1949	President	House passes
1950	President renews request	Senate passes—enacted
1951	Senate Finance Committee passes	House refuses
1952	President	passed
1953	President proposes new matching formula	not passed
1955	President resubmits request	no action
1956	President proposes medical changes	Senate adds benefit increase—passed
1958	Senate adds benefit increase	passed over presidential opposition
1959	President proposes reduction	Senate adds increase— dropped in conference
1960	Senate amendment for benefit increase	Defeated on Senate floor
1961	Senate adds increase	passed*
1962	House increases	passed*
1965		increased in Medicare bill
1967	Ways and Means Committee initiates	liberalized earnings requirements: tightened other AFDC requirements

*No AFDC increase.

and placed it squarely on the congressional agenda.[13] Within the Congress, changes in the composition of the House Agriculture Committee and rural-urban compromises on farm subsidy and food stamp issues were important in securing enactment of the programs.[14] The food stamp program has always been under the jurisdiction of the agriculture committees, while other nutrition programs for children and the elderly were shifted to the Education and Labor Committee in the House. All of these programs remain in the agriculture appropriations act and receive appropriations through the Appropriations Agriculture Subcommittee.

Presidential interest has been important in advancing and shaping the food stamp program. The actions of Presidents Eisenhower, Kennedy, Johnson, and Nixon all have had an effect on the program. The Eisenhower administration resisted efforts of some members of Congress to enact a program. Kennedy initiated the first pilot program. Johnson recommended the enactment of the first permanent program, and Nixon proposed the reforms enacted in 1970. The legislative committees and rural-urban compromises on farm policy were important congressional influences.

While the Democratic presidents Kennedy and Johnson supported efforts to make food stamps a national program to assist the poor, its transformation into one of the more costly and uniform national programs was furthered by the initiatives of a Republican president, Richard Nixon. In 1969 Nixon recommended doubling food stamps appropriations from $340 million to $610 million for FY70 and an increase to $1 billion for FY71. Included was a proposal of free stamps for the poor. While approved by the Senate, the bill met opposition from the conservative chairman of the House Agriculture Committee. The 1970 changes provided for $1.75 billion appropriation for FY71 and open-ended appropriations after that. More importantly, the bill required national eligibility and benefit standards. The 1970 amendments represented the first major modifications of the Food Stamp Act since its enactment in 1964. In subsequent enactments, Congress mandated participation by all counties. By 1980, the federal cost of food stamps was over $11 billion.

Since 1971, food stamp benefits have been set nationally and are indexed for food price increases. The benefit amounts are determined by both family size and income. The bonus value is the difference between the coupon face value and their purchase cost to the recipient. The family food allotment varies with family size; the purchase amount varies with income. The purchase requirement was eliminated by legislation in 1977.

The increases in program authorizations detailed in Table 7-8 illustrate the importance of a few program decisions on these

TABLE 7-8
Authorization for the Food Stamp Program, 1964–1982
(in billions of current dollars)

Year	President	Term	Amount per Year
1964	Johnson	3 years	$ .375 per year
1967	Johnson	2 years	.200 - 1968
			.225 - 1969
1968	Johnson	1 year	.315 - 1969
			.340 - 1970
			.170 - 1971 (½ year)
1969	Nixon	1 year	.610 - 1970
1970	Nixon	3 years	1.75 - 1971
			open - 1972
			open - 1973
1973	Nixon	4 years	open - 1974
			open - 1975
			open - 1976
			open - 1977
1977	Carter	4 years	5.85 - 1978
			6.16 - 1979
			6.19 - 1980
			6.24 - 1981
1979	Carter	1 year	6.78 - 1979
1980	Carter	2 years	9.5 - 1980
			9.7 - 1981
1981	Reagan	1 year	11.5 - 1981
1981	Reagan	1 year	−1.7 - 1982
1981	Reagan	1 year	11.3 - 1982
1982	Reagan	3 years	12.9 - 1983
			13.1 - 1984
			13.9 - 1985

expenditures. As Figure 7-1 shows, program growth was very slow until the expansion proposed by President Nixon. These changes set the basic food stamp allotment at $108 for a family of four regardless of income; before these changes the allotment varied from $60 to $120 depending on income. The purchase requirement for this four person family with the lowest income was reduced to $10 for $108 of stamps from the previous $20 for $85 of stamps. The change in the basic allotment and purchase

FIGURE 7-1
Growth in Food Stamp Expenditures, FY 1962–1985

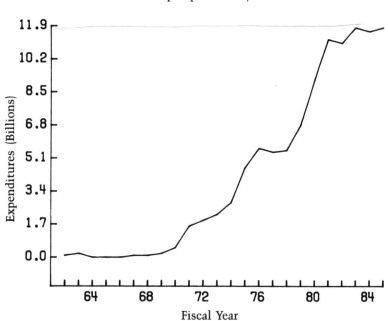

Source: *Historical Tables: Budget of the United States Government, Fiscal Year 1986.*

requirement dramatically increased benefits and resulting federal outlays. A report by the Congressional Budget Office noted that these changes transformed the food stamp program into "the first universal, national welfare program with national eligibility standards based on need and not on particular household characteristics."[15]

While the 1971 amendments increased benefits, the 1973 amendments increased participation by mandating that all areas of the country participate in the food stamp program. Prior to this, counties had the option of using food distribution rather than food stamps.

In terms of total outlays, these program adjustments had a

greater impact than the 1971 indexing provisions. From 1971 to
1976, benefits increased 54 percent due to increases in the price
of food. The total cost of these provisions was $0.5 billion, $1.1
billion, and $1.1 billion in 1978, 1979, and 1982 respectively.[16]
As Table 7-9 indicates, food prices rose more rapidly during this
period than did the broader consumer price indicator.

Additional authorization was repeatedly needed to keep expenditures at a level to meet demand. The rapid growth under
these changes and the open-ended authorization of 1973 resulted in efforts to curtail program growth in 1977. These
changes instituted semiannual price adjustments and eliminated the cash purchase price. The intent of these amendments

TABLE 7-9
Relationship between Food Stamp Benefits and Cost of Living
1971–1976

Year	Half[a]	Food[b]	All Items[b]	Monthly Food Stamp Allotment
1971	I	3.2	4.0	$108
1971	II	3.8	3.6	108
1972	I	4.2	3.0	108
1972	II	4.7	3.6	112
1973	I	16.2	5.9	112
1973	II	20.7	9.2	116
1974	I	14.7	10.6	142
1974	II	9.2	12.9	150
1975	I	8.0	8.3	154
1975	II	7.9	7.3	162
1976	I	1.2	4.9	166
1976	II	—	—	166

[a]First half of the year is indicated by I; second half is indicated by II.
[b]Entries are the percentage change from the preceding year at a com-
pound annual rate.

Source: "The Food Stamp Program: Income or Food Supplementation?," Budget
Issue Paper, Congressional Budget Office, Washington, D.C., Government Printing Office, 1977.

was to further concentrate benefits to the poor. The changes in eligibility reduced the rolls by one million people and reduced benefits for another three million. Under provisions which encouraged participation, however, additional low income persons were added to the rolls over the next two years. The open-ended authorization was removed, and a limit was placed on total expenditures. This limit, as Table 7-8 illustrates, was subsequently adjusted upward to meet caseload demands.

VETERANS' BENEFITS

The pattern of increases for the cash programs in veterans' benefits reflects relatively noncontroversial benefit increases to keep pace with price increases and with increases in social security benefits. Because pension benefits are income tested, an increase in social security benefits without a comparable increase in pension benefits results in lower benefits to pension recipients.[17] Many of the pension benefit increases were passed following increases in social security benefits. Congress, however, did resist tying these two actions together automatically. Legislation enacted in 1978 finally did legislate the relationship between social security and veterans' pensions.

The relationship between the minimum pension benefit and the cost of living index is shown in Table 7-10. The figures show an almost 600 percent increase in pensions since 1933, while the consumer price index has increased 357 percent. Examining these figures more closely one can see that between 1952 and 1977, benefits and prices have increased at nearly the same rate if the 1960 increases are ignored. The 1960 increases raised the absolute level of benefits. Since that time, the change in benefits and prices has once again been close. Pensions have increased 109 percent while the CPI has increased 96.5 percent.

Benefit increases have generally originated in the House Veterans Committee or have been requested by Democratic presi-

TABLE 7-10
Relationship between Veterans' Benefits and Cost of Living,
1933–1977

Effective Date	Monthly Benefits[a]	CPI[b]	Benefit Change[c]	CPI Change[d]
July 1933	$30.00	$38.1	— %	— %
June 1942	40.00	48.8	33.3	28.1
May 1944	50.00	52.4	66.6	37.5
September 1946	60.00	60.5	100.0	58.8
July 1952	63.00	70.5	110.0	108.7
October 1954	66.15	80.4	120.5	111.0
July 1960	100.00	88.7	233.3	132.8
January 1966	115.00	93.6	233.3	145.7
October 1967	119.00	100.7	296.7	164.3
January 1969	130.00	106.4	333.3	179.3
January 1971	142.00	119.1	373.3	212.6
January 1972	150.00	123.1	400.0	223.1
January 1974	164.00	138.5	446.7	263.5
January 1975	182.00	155.4	506.7	307.9
January 1976	196.00	166.3	553.3	336.5
January 1977	209.00	174.3	596.7	357.5

[a]Entries are nonservice connected pension benefits, calculated as minimum income for veterans and three dependents.
[b]Consumer price index 1967 = 100.
[c]Percent change in monthly pension rates over July 1933 rate.
[d]Percent change in cost of living index over that for July 1933.

Source: Committee on Veterans Affairs, United States Senate, Committee Print 13 (Jan. 30, 1978), 95th Congress, 2nd Session.

dents as cost of living adjustments. As with social security, veterans' benefit increases have often exceeded both the president's request and the cost of living increase. President Johnson had the most legislative success with his proposals. In 1964, the Senate scaled back the House increase to match the president's wishes and in 1967 passed his proposed 5.4 percent adjustment without change. The Democratic Congress increased compensation over presidential wishes in 1957, 1962, and 1975.[18]

INDEXING ADOPTION, 1969–1980

Prior to 1969 the pattern of *ad hoc* benefit adjustments became routine. Cash programs followed the lead of social security. The recommendations of the Social Security Advisory Councils usually set the stage for election year increases endorsed by the House Ways and Means Committee and bid up by the Democratic congresses. In their first terms presidents assisted through their benefit adjustment recommendations. The Senate usually attached provisions for public assistance benefits. This was followed by adjustments to veterans' pensions for the social security increases. Concern for rising AFDC costs and welfare dependency in the late sixties tended to distinguish that program as a costly welfare program not in congressional favor.

A combination of events brought about the wave of indexing in 1969–1980. These were concerns about inflation, Republican policy initiatives, and an erosion of the Ways and Means Committee's control over social security. Inflation was never a serious problem until the years following 1968. From 1952 to 1967, annual changes in the CPI never exceeded 4.0 percent as the four-year averages in Table 7-11 reveal. Inflation, however, was not the prime motivation for enacting indexing. Some conservatives saw it as a way to hold down the increasingly popular and timely *ad hoc* increases. Social security administrators saw it as a way to minimize lags between inflation and *ad hoc* increases. Liberals saw it as a way to insure benefit increases that could occasionally be supplemented.[19]

Republican leaders on the Ways and Means Committee had long favored automatic increases to the *ad hoc* adjustments controlled by the Ways and Means Committee chairman, Wilbur Mills, and by the Social Security Administration. Automatic adjustments were part of both the Republican and Democratic party platforms in 1968 and were repeatedly proposed by President Nixon.

Political scientists are almost universally familiar with the descriptions of the roles and respect attributed to the Ways and

TABLE 7-11
Average Changes in the Consumer Price Index during Presidential
Administrations, 1949–1984

		Average	Low	High
1949–52	Truman	2.5	−1.0	7.9
1953–56	Eisenhower I	0.6	−0.4	1.5
1957–60	Eisenhower II	2.2	0.8	3.6
1961–64	Kennedy–Johnson	1.2	1.0	1.3
1965–68	Johnson	2.9	1.7	4.2
1969–72	Nixon	4.7	3.3	5.9
1973–76	Nixon–Ford	8.0	5.8	11.0
1977–80	Carter	9.8	6.5	13.5
1981–84*	Reagan I	6.3	4.2	10.4

*1983 and 1984 based on estimates from president's fiscal 1985 budget.

Note: Average of year to year changes in the CPI (all items). Low and high are the extreme years for each administration.

Source: Economic Report of the President, 1983.

Means Committee and its members.[20] The recommendations of the committee were usually reported to the floor under closed rules which permitted no amendments. Congress was generally satisfied that the committee knew best how to handle tax and trust fund issues. Member interest was accommodated within the committee in order to continue to receive this support. John Manley describes how Wilbur Mills suffered one defeat on the House floor in 1958 shortly after becoming chairman.[21] The committee reported a bill to pay unemployment benefits to workers who had not fully earned them under existing unemployment statutes. This was considered a welfare addition to the insurance program and was rejected by the House. This defeat is often cited as influencing Mills in his subsequent handling of Ways and Means Committee matters. It is notable that the decision of the House to index social security benefits was the second major rejection for Chairman Mills over ten years later.[22]

In accepting the indexing provision for social security in 1970, the House first modified the rules to permit amendments and then amended the Ways and Means Committee bill to provide for automatic increases when the cost of living exceeds 3 percent in the previous year. Ways and Means Committee members were divided on the amendment, which was sponsored by the committee's ranking Republican member, John Byrnes. The bill ultimately failed when Mills refused to go to conference at the end of the year.

The enactment of the indexing provision occurred in 1972 when it was coupled with a 20 percent increase in social security benefits. The initiative for this measure arose in the Senate as an amendment to the public debt ceiling. Mills had earlier introduced a similar bill in the House. The measure was not considered by the Ways and Means Committee but was adopted on the House floor. Some attribute Mills's change of heart to his 1972 presidential aspirations.[23]

While the 1972 social security increase of 20 percent was opposed by Nixon, he nonetheless capitalized on the increase, which was paid just prior to the election. All social security recipients received an insert from the president with their checks informing them of the increase. In 1973, Congress twice revised the automatic provision to modify the timing of the benefit adjustments. The 1977 amendments corrected an error in the formula that had resulted in some retirees receiving benefit increases greater than the CPI increase and revised the earnings and benefit formulas. With inflation heating up, the indexing provision became very costly. The estimated cost of indexing was $6.6 billion in 1978; $8.5 billion in 1979; and $16.8 billion in 1980. These costs become compounded with each future year.

Many of the changes in social programs during the Nixon administration were affected by the congressional debate over the president's proposed Family Assistance Plan. Congress could never reach agreement on the AFDC program but did create a federal Supplemental Security Income plan out of the existing federal-state programs for the aged, the blind, and the disabled. This program was enacted in 1972 and was to be effective in January 1974. Benefits were adjusted twice before the program went into effect. Since SSI benefits are reduced dollar per dollar for social security increases, these increases provided only a net increase to recipients of 4.3 percent. Seven months after the program took effect, Congress indexed the benefits so that they were adjusted with social security benefits. A year later, Congress required that the states pass these increases along to the recipients and not simply absorb the increased federal contributions. This is referred to as the "mandatory pass-through" provision. The cost of the automatic SSI provisions was $295 million in 1978 and $380 million in 1980.

Between 1969 and 1980, Congress indexed more and more provisions of social programs. Because of the overlapping nature of federal programs, it was necessary to adjust eligibility and income conditions of programs simultaneously. Otherwise a person might lose benefits from one program because their income increased due to benefit adjustments of another program. With inflation running at high levels during this period, these automatic adjustments were the easiest way to pass along benefit increases to the poor. Only one major program remained unindexed after this period. This program is the primary program people think of when they mention welfare: it is the AFDC program. This lack of AFDC indexing was the casualty of Congress's failure to adopt the Nixon Family Assistance Plan. Congress also did not pass Carter's welfare reform. Thus, federal contributions for AFDC have not been adjusted since 1967. Some states have independently chosen to adjust their share and individual benefits.

With the emphasis that members of Congress increasingly place on credit taking and the provisions of programs which benefit their constituencies, some might wonder why Congress would enact automatic benefit adjustments rather than continuing to provide *ad hoc* adjustments for which they take credit. We argue here that conservatives saw it as a way to limit these generous *ad hoc* increases and liberals saw them as a floor which might be added to. Once social security was indexed, others sought to put similar benefit programs on a equal footing as well as to avoid having to adjust other interconnected programs individually at the same time.

The liberal benefit adjustments to the Civil Service pensions was not lost on advocates of indexing. These pensions had been indexed since 1962 and in the 1970s received twice a year adjustments with a provision which added 1 percent plus the change in CPI. The automatic adjustment for social security became an expected benefit increase that members would later take credit for protecting.

SCALING DOWN INDEXING, 1981–1984

When the Reagan administration took office, inflation and the indexed provisions had pushed the cost of indexing to very high levels. Table 7-12 shows the overall costs to the federal treasury of the major indexed programs. Costs were projected to

TABLE 7-12
Cost Increases of Indexed Provisions
(in millions of dollars)

	FY 1978	FY 1979	FY 1982
Social Security—Old Age, Survivors, and Disability	$6,600	$8,500	$18,800
Civil Service Retirement	500	800	1,400
Railroad Retirement	225	359	600
Military Retirement	537	734	1,200
Veterans' Pensions	0	26	300
Food Stamps	500	1,100	1,147
Unemployment, Extended Benefits	1,266	428	3,117
Total	$9,628	$11,947	$26,564

Source: *Indexation of Federal Programs*, p. 15.

almost triple over the next four years.[24] The 1981 Reconciliation Act delayed cost of living adjustments (COLA) for food stamps. This and other changes were estimated to reduce food stamp expenditures by $1.7 billion. The other change in COLA provisions in the Reconciliation Act was a change in federal pensions. In 1982 the COLA for SSI was limited. The 1983 social security financing changes delayed the cost of living adjustment six months and made future adjustments effective in January. The FY84 Reagan budget requested similar six month delays in the SSI, food stamp, child nutrition programs. The president also recommended decoupling some housing programs from automatic responsiveness to market conditions. The cost of all of these provisions represented uncontrollable savings which could be used to reduce the growing federal budget.

The expansionary period of federal social spending was coming to an end. The Reagan administration placed new emphasis on concerns over indexing costs and uncontrollable aspects of the budget. Even with inflation slowing down, the total costs of the social insurance components of the budget represented opportunity for cost saving by modifying indexing provisions.

8

Politics and Social Welfare Policy

Much has been written on the subject of social welfare policy. It is a topic which interests scholars from many disciplines. With time and a wide range of studies we are approaching the point at which we can confidently say that we understand the forces which have shaped the multiple programs which constitute U.S. social policy. From a political perspective we can also begin to more fully understand how the range and choice of policies pursued by the federal government result from the political control of the Congress and the presidency and from the interaction of these institutions with economic conditions. We can also move ahead to examine critical questions which remained unanswered. These questions involve the linkage of conditions of political control with policy impacts. How, we can now ask, have political forces affected the economic well-being of individual groups?

PRESIDENTIAL EFFECTS ON POLICY

An important finding illuminated in this study is that periods of Republican control of the presidency have been the years when federal social welfare expenditures have increased the most in real terms. Two notable exceptions to this pattern exist:

the Johnson presidency, when expenditures grew, and the Reagan presidency, when expenditures declined. During the other seven administrations between fiscal 1950 and 1985, growth during Republican administrations has exceeded growth during the Democratic administrations. This finding applies only to social welfare expenditures, not to the budget as a whole. Republican presidents usually were successful in controlling expenditures for nonsocial welfare expenditures and for the total budget. Expenditures for social programs diverged from the widely accepted view of presidents and policy that Democratic presidents promote social welfare spending.

One important reason for this pattern is the cycle of unemployment. Unemployment has exhibited a trend of increasing during Republican administrations and declining during Democratic administrations. The late Carter and early Reagan administrations are the exceptions to this rule. In other administrations unemployment is higher when a Republican president leaves office and lower when a Democratic president leaves office. Unemployment exerts a direct, immediate, and positive effect on social welfare expenditures increasing these expenditures on the order of 5 to 6 percent in real terms for each 1 percent increase in unemployment.

PRESIDENTS AND CONGRESS

Presidents do not affect policy in a political vacuum. The party and size of the congressional margins influence the success of presidents in affecting social welfare expenditures. We do see that presidents have initiated more new social welfare programs than has the Congress. Overall, more policies have been initiated during Democratic control of Congress and the presidency than during any other combination of institutional conrol. Most of the initiations of new programs occurred during the Kennedy and Johnson presidencies. Congress continued to initiate new programs through the Nixon administration. After this, the number of new programs falls off considerably.

The party of Congress is an important influence. Democrats, who tend to create new in-kind programs, require sufficient numbers of House nonsouthern Democrats to have an effect on social programs. During Republican presidencies, the Democratic Congress will meet and raise any presidential initiatives to increase cash benefits. This, plus the unemployment effect, has helped to drive social expenditures upward during Republican administrations.

For Democratic presidents to achieve success with their initiatives, they need to affect the control of congressional committees and overcome long standing congressional opposition to many of the reforms and new programs they are initiating. The size of the congressional margin is what differentiates the Kennedy administration from the Johnson administration. Kennedy made his share of recommendations. He did not have the support and margins in key committees and in the Congress as a whole to achieve the success that Johnson realized.

DIFFERENCES IN TYPES OF PROGRAMS

While the term social welfare is commonly used, it encompasses much. Social welfare includes cash as well as in-kind expenditures. It includes social insurance, public assistance, food, housing, health, and veterans programs. Education, manpower, and social services programs also are an important part of the nation's social welfare effort. These programs vary in their target beneficiaries and conditions of assistance, but they vary in the conditions that influence their growth as well.

The older social insurance programs are the most favored. They have been adjusted most often and have grown to be the largest component of federal social welfare spending. It is these programs which have grown during Republican administrations. Part of this growth is due to the effects of unemployment. Part is due to the first term social security adjustments recommended by presidents. Election year increases have also contributed and have at times been bid upward by the Democratic congresses trying to outdo the Republican president.

Cash public assistance programs have not been so favored. In the 1950s and up until the mid-1960s public assistance benefits were adjusted with social security benefits. The concern over rising AFDC and dependency upon these benefits left the federal contribution for AFDC benefits unadjusted since 1967. AFDC remains the sole federal cash assistance program which is not indexed directly or indirectly for price changes. The cash programs for the deserving poor—the programs for poor blind, aged, or disabled—were consolidated into a national program and have been indexed. Modifications of the public assistance programs were proposed by Democratic presidents or by Congress during the Eisenhower administration. President Nixon sought far reaching reforms under his Family Assistance Program proposal. The reforms of the AFDC program were not adopted when the other public assistance categories were restructured.

Democratic presidents have pushed expansion of the in-kind programs. The food, housing, and health programs were established as permanent programs with substantial funding during the Johnson presidency. Each of these were pushed by President Kennedy and prior to that by liberal Democrats in Congress. President Carter is an exception among the Democrats for not expanding in-kind programs.

The impact of the Democratic presidents is also seen with the programs which are not in the income security category. The education, manpower, and social service programs expanded under the Democratic presidents. It is with these programs that the immediate impact of the Democratic presidents is observed. The break between the Nixon and Johnson presidencies is seen in this category and not in the income security category. The

Nixon presidency moved away from the War on Poverty focus on education, community activism, and social services and toward the programs of the income security category.

Veterans are a category favored by Congress. Adjustments for veterans' pensions have been made to keep them in pace with price changes and changes in the social security program with which these benefits are interdependent. Veterans programs do exhibit a cyclical pattern related to American wars. Veterans' income security benefits have been kept separate and adjusted as a sign of the special status of veterans in society. Presidents have sought unsuccessfully to revise or limit increases in some of these programs.

PERIODS OF POLICY CHANGE

There are some distinct periods of change in emphasis that can be observed throughout the years we examine. President Truman had modest success in his social welfare efforts. He did succeed with his request for social security increases and in effect placed social security in a position which made it difficult for President Eisenhower to modify or scale down the program. This had been a platform proposal of the Republican party for some time. Truman did not succeed with other proposals for health or disability insurance.

The Eisenhower years were marked by congressional expansion of social programs. Eisenhower's requests were modest. He succeeded somewhat in slowing government growth but not social programs. His proposals to reduce federal public assistance contributions were ignored throughout his second term, and federal shares were increased by the Congress. Late in the second term, education expenditures were increased in response to the Soviet launch of the Sputnik satellite. Unemployment triggered increased expenditures in the second term and helped elect sufficient numbers of Democrats to the Congress to pass some new programs.

President Kennedy did bring a new agenda. He proposed programs for food stamps, for education, housing, social services, and manpower. He succeeded in some public assistance reform proposals. Johnson succeeded where Kennedy failed. The health and education successes were programs that had been recommended but failed to clear Congress in the preceding years. The housing initiatives brought new programs. The most innovative aspect of this administration was its implementation of new programs under Title II of the Economic Opportunity Act. The programs created under this authority by executive order were later earmarked by Congress for funding under OEO authorization and subsequently many became separately funded programs. What differed in the Kennedy and Johnson terms was the scale of the programs and what was possible with the increased Democratic margins enjoyed by Johnson in the Congress.

As mentioned previously, the break between the Nixon and Johnson administrations was in the education, manpower, and social service programs.[1] Nixon sought to end OEO programs and to reduce expenditures in education. He sought expansions of food stamps and reform of public assistance. He recommended free food stamps. Nixon advocated indexing of social security benefits from his first year on, but he did sign and take credit for the 20 percent increase in social security benefits prior to the 1972 election. Nixon succeeded in another area which had eluded every previous president. Unemployment benefit coverage was expanded. Some expansion had been recommended by every president annually from Truman to Johnson.

A break did come with the Johnson policies in the second Nixon term. The second term recommendations of Nixon and then the recommendations of Ford, of Carter, and of Reagan all were designed to slow the growth of social spending. Until the Reagan presidency the Congress resisted many of these recommendations. Spending did slow and, in many respects, the Carter presidency looked like Republican presidencies. It is during the Reagan presidency that programs are cut and actually decline in real terms.

The three distinct periods which we observe are the congressional expansion of social insurance during the Eisenhower presidency; the enactment of new in-kind programs during the Kennedy, Johnson, and Nixon terms; and finally the post-Nixon period of trying to check growth of in-kind programs. The New Deal programs were adjusted upward and expanded in the 1950s, and a new set of programs was put in place in the 1960s and added to during the next Republican administration. Ford did not succeed with the major restructuring he proposed. It was during the second Nixon term that indexing was fully implemented and that public works programs to combat unemployment were enacted. The combination of double digit inflation and rising unemployment pushed social spending and the Democratic Congress toward expanded programs.

President Carter made modest proposals. His first budget was marked by a dramatic shift from the priorities of the Ford budget which was pending before the Congress. This first budget revision paralleled that of President Kennedy who sought to modify the no-expansion Eisenhower budget which was pending after Kennedy's inauguration. Carter's subsequent budgets did not seek many expansions.

It was President Reagan who sought and achieved the most significant cuts in social spending. The trend was downward when he took office. Major savings were proposed in just about every area of social spending. Many of these proposals were enacted early in the administration.

ENTITLEMENTS AND CONTROLLABLE SPENDING

Throughout the entire period of this analysis, we have been studying the growth in entitlement spending. Every president has sought to modify legislation affecting spending in the annual submissions of legislation to the Congress. The post-Johnson presidents, for example, all sought some way to control health costs. Few presidents were successful in achieving many reductions in entitlements prior to Reagan. Presidents may have complained that expenditures were uncontrollable, but it was usually not for lack of effort on their part. The Reagan changes in social spending do merit additional discussion.

A NEW PRESIDENT AND NEW PRIORITIES: RONALD REAGAN

This analysis of previous spending decisions provides a perspective to understand the priorities of the Reagan administration, which came into office committed to stemming the increases in federal social welfare spending. Approximately 75 percent of the federal budget was termed "relatively uncontrollable" indicating that spending would continue at that level unless Congress altered existing laws and previous commitments. Spending for social programs consumed over half of the $700 billion budget. To an administration philosophically opposed to many of these social programs and with its own priorities to increase the defense budget and lower taxes, cuts in social programs were a major priority.

In a very early policy document, budget director David Stockman indicated that he knew where he would achieve the social welfare savings. Setting aside social security, which he wrote "would be a political disaster to tinker with in the first round,"[2] he zeroed in on the nonsocial security entitlements. In the so-called Dunkirk paper of December 1980 he wrote: "Current expenditures for food stamps, cash assistance, Medicaid, disability, heating assistance, WIC [Women, Infant, and Children Food Program], school lunches, and unemployment compensation amount to $100 billion. A carefully tailored package to reduce eligibility, overlap, and abuse should be developed for these areas—with potential savings of $10–20 billion."[3]

The 1981 Omnibus Budget Reconciliation Act did implement cuts in many of these programs. The importance of this bill was that it changed many existing laws and altered many statutory eligibility criteria for de facto entitlement programs. A fiscal year 1982 budget savings of $35.2 billion was projected from the cuts made in seventeen federal programs.[4] These cuts primarily altered the liberalized eligibility requirements and benefit adjustments enacted in the 1970–1976 period. For programs such as Pell grants for education, CETA job training, WIC, energy assistance, and Title XX services a cap was placed on total expenditures to reduce program costs. Federal program contributions to Medicaid and school nutrition programs were reduced. Eligibility was restricted for food stamps and school lunches while benefits for AFDC recipients were reduced. Two programs—CETA public works jobs (Title 6) and the social security minimum benefit—were eliminated.

Throughout this debate, the administration emphasized its support for the "safety net"—those programs targeted to those who "rely on government for their very existence."[5] These programs were identified as social security, Medicare, Veterans' pensions and compensation, Supplemental Security Income, Head Start, summer jobs for disadvantaged youths, and free school lunches and breakfasts. This emphasis reinforced the concept of a federal welfare commitment to the elderly, the veterans, and the destitute. Those who were barely above the poverty line, or who were only above the poverty line by virtue of the federal in-kind benefits they received, would bear the brunt of the cuts in nonsocial security entitlements. While seeking to end benefits to those who could pay, the Reagan cuts fell the hardest on the working poor.[6]

Most important from the standpoint of this analysis is to understand that the Reagan administration priorities were not targeted primarily at War on Poverty programs, but at the expansion of the welfare state realized in the post-Johnson years. Most of these eligibility changes and new programs were enacted during the Nixon and Ford presidencies. Nixon had already done battle with the War on Poverty, and the original OEO programs had been modified and placed under new auspices. The increases in program benefits of the safety net programs were also enacted in the post-Johnson years. Although the poor, and especially the elderly poor, have benefited from these increases, the bulk of the safety net programs (social security, Medicare, and veterans' benefits) are not specifically targeted to the poor.[7]

Originally the public assistance categories were expected to wither away. As more of the elderly and disabled were insured under social security provisions and assisted further by in-kind services such as training, housing, nutrition, and social services, these categories did dwindle and the economic well-being of recipients improved. The same phenomenon did not occur with the public assistance program commonly thought of as welfare—AFDC. This program grew rather than shrunk. It was also dependent upon states to implement federal changes and raise benefits. This did not readily occur in many states.

POLICY OUTCOMES AND POLICY IMPACTS

The antipoverty effects of the various social welfare policy instruments vary as do their growth rates. Robert Plotnick has estimated that 55 percent of all federal social programs were paid to the pre-transfer poor in 1974. Table 8-1 shows the percentage of benefits received by the pre-transfer poor in some of the major program categories we have been considering. The poor receive slightly over half of all federal cash income transfers. While not targeted to the poor, programs such as social security transfer more income to the poor than do targeted programs such as the cash public assistance programs. The dollars in the public assistance program are a mere fraction of total cash transfers.

Similarly, more dollars are received by the poor under the in-kind programs than the cash public assistance programs. More money is spent on low income in-kind programs than on cash low income programs and a relatively high percentage of all in-kind programs are received by the poor. Medicaid and food stamps are the largest in-kind transfer programs for the poor.

TABLE 8-1
Percentage of Assistance to Pre-transfer Poor
under Federal Programs, 1974

Cash Transfers	55.0%
Social Security	58.8
Unemployment Insurance	20.8
Public Assistance	85.9
Veterans Income Security	43.0
In-kind transfers	
Food Stamps	71%
Child Nutrition	83
Housing	65
Health	58
Medicare	59
Medicaid	73
Social Services	69
Employment and Manpower	70
Manpower Training	86
Education	30

Source: Robert D. Plotnick, "Social Welfare Expenditures and the Poor," *Policy Analysis* 5 (Summer
1979): 271–90. Used with permission.

Even the manpower training programs, which were an early
component of the War on Poverty and which grew even larger in
the 1970s, pay a high percentage of their benefits to the poor.

The importance of the nonmeans tested cash transfer payments is reinforced by an analysis by Danziger and Plotnick. As
Table 8-2 illustrates, six times more persons have been removed
from poverty through cash social insurance transfers than
through public assistance cash programs. During the decade
following the declaration of the War on Poverty the percentage
of persons removed from poverty by income tested cash transfers doubled, but this 3 percent change pales by comparison to
the 14 percent change observed in the effect of cash insurance
transfers. In-kind transfers have also removed more persons
from poverty than have cash transfers directed toward the poor.

The poor are better off because all persons have gained under
nonmeans programs. The growth we have observed in the social

TABLE 8-2
Percentage of Pre-transfer Poor Removed from Poverty by Type of
Program, 1965–1978

	Cash Social Insurance[1]	Cash Public Assistance[2]	In-kind Transfers[3]	All Transfers
Absolute				
1965	23.5	3.3	16.4	43.2
1976	37.6	6.2	28.1	71.9
1978	37.6	5.9	—	—
Relative				
1965	23.5	3.3	—	—
1976	32.4	3.7	—	—

[1] Cash social insurance programs include social security, railroad retirement, unemployment compensation, workmen's compensation, government employee pensions, and veterans' pensions and compensation.

[2] Cash public assistance transfers include AFDC, SSI (OAD, APTD, and AB in 1965) and General Assistance.

[3] In-kind transfers include Medicare, Medicaid, food stamps, and, for 1976, school lunch and public housing; this figure also adjusts for direct taxes and the underreporting of cash transfers.

Source: Sheldon Danziger and Robert Plotnick, "The War on Poverty: Achievements and Failures" in *Welfare Reform in America*, ed. Paul M. Sommers (Boston: Kluwer-Nijhoff, 1982). Used with permission.

insurance and in-kind programs have had the most impact in reducing the numbers of persons who are post-transfer poor. The major growth in the nonmeans social insurance programs has had important effect on the reduction of poverty. Robert Plotnick observes on a decade of antipoverty developments.

> The poor's total benefits rose by $71 billion during 1965–1974. Income tested programs accounted for one third of this growth. The remainder came from programs available to persons of all income classes and quietly grew, apart from the continuing debates over the war on poverty, welfare reform, and other specific antipoverty measures.[8]

The irony is that it is the growth of the social insurance programs seen in the Republican administrations that have had the most effect in reducing poverty. Previous studies of social spending across nations show that expenditures for social welfare increase with the economic development of the nation and the countries with older social programs have tended to have a larger share of the national product devoted to those expenditures. The findings here are consistent with these general findings. Gradual expansion by including more persons within the social insurance programs and increased benefits under these programs push social spending upward. Previously, Republicans taking office have not tried to alter the basic nature of the social insurance programs.[9] They have promoted lower levels of spending by targeting benefits of some programs toward the poor. They have also favored broader coverage under social insurance programs over the cash public assistance programs.

CONCLUSION

The analysis contained in this book points to the implications of party government and our system of institutional checks and balances for policy. Control of the Congress by the Democratic party has been accompanied by increases in spending for social programs. Contrary to the common argument that divided party control of the Congress and the presidency is a stalemate condition, this study reveals that it is during these periods that social welfare spending has increased. Both total expenditures and cash expenditures have increased during these periods. The impetus for these increases may have been the interest of the Democratic party to counter the policy objectives of the Republican president.

Economic conditions have provided the impetus for adjustments in cash benefit programs, but it has been the political calendar that has regularized the increases. The policy agenda for new presidents has always included some benefit adjustments for social security. Congress has made additional adjustments to social security benefits and to other benefit programs with which the president has been less generous. The occurrence of elections has stimulated these benefit increases. So while price increases have created the justifications for benefit increases, it is the political calendar which has promoted their enactment and the political composition their size.

These findings support the idea that social welfare policy is multi-dimensional. Previous analyses have relied on social welfare policy as a policy classification which unifies policies of a similar nature. From the discussion in chapter four, it can be seen that there are many differences in types and conditions of assistance within social welfare policy. Policies using the budget categories, cash - in-kind distinctions, payments to individuals and major programs have been analyzed.

We do find that the effect of political and economic influences varies with the type of policy. We have seen that the presidential interest has not been as strong with other benefit programs as it has been with social security. The Senate often took the initiative in pushing public assistance benefit increases. Presidents of both parties resisted increases in veterans' pension benefits. In total, congressional support for cash benefits has been strong and bipartisan. The benefits of categorical assistance programs are old programs which are readily susceptible to "tireless tinkering," to use Steiner's phrase. They are the stable cash component of social welfare expenditures which can be easily adjusted. Inflation provides a ready justification.

Diverging from the cash programs is the noncash component. These have been the new programs which represent the innovations of the War on Poverty and related efforts to combat poverty and increase economic opportunity. Congressional and presidential interest in these noncash programs follows traditional party lines. Nonsouthern Democrats have been an important policy influence. These noncash programs are not affected by economic conditions as are the cash programs. In these programs, the regularity of the political calendar or of economic events have been less important than have been the changes in party control or the composition of Congress.

This analysis does not account for the origin of the U.S. social welfare state but does show factors contributing to its development and direction. Studies which describe the origin of social programs or compare expenditures of developed countries might label this policy process as an incremental one. Certainly this is true of present U.S. programs and of nations which have stable political institutions and benefit programs legislated and appropriated for multi-year periods. Attributing spending for current programs only to spending for previous programs is insufficient as an explanation of the process. This analysis has shown the importance of political factors in influencing social spending beyond that of the previous year. It has also shown that in addition to stable programs, there are occasional dramatic increases in spending arising from new programs or program expansion. These new programs are usually not radical innovations and oftentimes have been on the policy agenda for some time prior to enactment.

The last quarter century has been a period of steady expansion of the U.S. welfare state. The insurance programs of the New Deal have been expanded to pay benefits to workers and dependents in cases of loss of earning ability. Medical benefits to these persons were added after a long struggle which culminated only after the election of 1964. Some extensions of benefits have also resulted from court decisions. The major innovations and expansion of social welfare have been in noncash programs. Cash supplements and guaranteed income proposals have received much less support than has in-kind assistance. In-kind programs have grown rapidly during certain periods.

This emphasis on conditions of assistance has implications for who benefits from social programs. For those defined as categorically eligible—primarily workers, their dependents, the disabled, and veterans—the combination of economic and political events has insured their continued and increased benefits.

The public assistance programs have increasingly received more critical attention as evidenced by the enactment of training requirements and concern about absent parents. The working poor have had fewer benefit programs. Expansion of benefits and eligibility conditions has generally followed Democratic presidents and increases in the number of nonsouthern Democrats. These patterns of expenditures and benefit conditions lie at the heart of the question of "who gets what" and are directly related to the distribution of income. Policy outcomes and impacts follow from the partisan control of government and the margins in Congress. Measuring these policy outcomes and linking them to measures of political factors allows us to address an important political question: that is, how does the constitutional and party system affect the design and distribution of social welfare benefits?

From this analysis we can also ask what we have learned about the policy process and the study of public policy. Public policy making is certainly multi-faceted. Neither political institutional factors nor policy measurement can be ignored. How these policy components are integrated with the institutional components needs careful consideration. It is necessary to reemphasize and integrate these institutional processes into policy models rather than ignoring them as is oftentimes done. This requires attention to measurement both of policy and policy influences, and the careful specification of relationships between them.

Examining the individual factors which have influenced social spending and how the individual components have evolved into the current mix of social programs still leaves us short of a comprehensive explanation. Party competition and divided congressional jurisdiction lead to a series of new programs and expansions of existing programs. The fragmentation of the policy process results in fragmentation of the policies. Major reforms are rare. More often, small changes result in large program changes over time as individual behavior responds to economic conditions and modified eligibility and benefit conditions. Over time, the overlapping programs are integrated through related eligibility conditions.

These questions take on particular importance today as we assess the slowdown in the growth of programs and the future responsiveness to political changes. Much more needs to be done in developing policy outcome and impact measures which will better enable us to assess how benefits received, income, and well-being are affected by political parties and economic conditions. This type of analysis can be integrated with economic studies assessing benefit impact.

Notes

CHAPTER 1

1. All social welfare expenditures cited in this chapter are taken from the Social Security Administration series. See Alma McMillan and Ann Kallman Bixby, "Social Welfare Expenditures, Fiscal Year 1978," *Social Security Bulletin* 43 (May 1980):3–17, and Ann Kallman Bixby, "Social Welfare Expenditures, Fiscal Year 1980," *Social Security Bulletin* 46 (Aug. 1983):9–17. See also U.S. Department of Health, Education and Welfare, *Social Welfare Expenditures under Public Programs in the United States, 1929–1966,* Research Report no 25. Social Security Administration (Washington, D.C.: Government Printing Office, 1968).

2. Political science studies of social programs are fairly well typified by studies such as Gilbert Y. Steiner, *The State of Welfare* (Washington, D.C.: Brookings Institution, 1971); Martha Derthick, *Policymaking for Social Security* (Washington, D.C.: Brookings Institution, 1979); and Daniel P. Moynihan, *The Politics of a Guaranteed Income* (New York: Vintage Books, 1973).

3. The reform literature includes works such as Michael C. Barth, George J. Carcagno, and John L. Palmer, *Toward an Effective Income Support System: Problems, Prospects and Choices* (Madison, Wisc.: Institute for Research on Poverty, 1974); Martin Anderson, *Welfare* (Stanford, Calif.: Hoover Institution Press, 1978); *Welfare Reform in America,* ed. Paul M. Sommers (Boston: Kluwer-Nijhoff Publishing, 1982).

4. Economic studies have analyzed characteristics of individual beneficiaries. See, e.g., Robert Lampman, *Ends and Means of Reducing Income Poverty* (New York: Academic Press, 1971) and

Robert D. Plotnick and Felicity Skidmore, *Progress Against Poverty* (New York: Academic Press, 1975) for analyses of characteristics of program recipients. Also see studies published by the Social Security Administration in *Social Security Bulletin*. Page has examined the distributional impact of a wide range of government policies. See Benjamin I. Page, *Who Gets What from Government* (Berkeley: Univ. of California Press, 1983).

5. For accounts of recent developments and growth of social programs, see *A Decade of Federal Antipoverty Programs*, ed. Robert H. Haveman (New York: Academic Press, 1977); Sar A. Levitan and Robert Taggart, *The Promise of Greatness* (Cambridge, Mass.: Harvard Univ. Press, 1976); and Sar A. Levitan, *Programs in Aid of the Poor for the 1980's*, 4th ed. (Baltimore: Johns Hopkins Univ. Press, 1980).

6. McMillan and Bixby, "Social Welfare Expenditures, Fiscal Year 1978," *Social Security Bulletin* 43:3–17, esp. p. 3.

7. For a history of the provisions of the Social Security Act, see Edwin E. Witte, *The Development of the Social Security Act* (Madison: Univ. of Wisconsin Press, 1963); Arthur J. Altmeyer, *The Formative Years of Social Security* (Madison: Univ. of Wisconsin Press, 1966). For an excellent analysis of later developments, see Derthick, *Policymaking for Social Security*.

8. For an historical analysis of approaches to poverty and welfare in the United States, see James T. Patterson, *America's Struggle Against Poverty 1900–1980* (Cambridge, Mass.: Harvard Univ. Press, 1981).

9. See Steiner, *The State of Welfare*, ch. 7.

10. All figures are taken from Sheldon Danziger and Robert Plotnick, "The War on Income Poverty: Achievements and Failures" in *Welfare Reform in America*, ed. Sommers, 31–52.

11. Report of the House Select Committee on Aging quoted in "How Poor are the Elderly?," *New York Times*, Dec. 19, 1982.

12. *Studies in Public Welfare*, Paper no. 2, "Handbook of Public Income Transfer Programs," U.S. Joint Economic Committee, 92nd Congress, 2nd Session, Oct. 16, 1972, p. 1.

13. See, e.g., Irwin Garfinkel and Robert Haveman, "Income Transfer Policy in the United States: A Review and Assessment," Discussion Paper #701-82 (Madison, Wisc.: Institute for Research on Poverty, 1982). See also welfare reform literature cited above.

14. See Robert Lampman, "What Does it Do for the Poor? A New Test for National Policy," *Public Interest* 34 (Winter 1974): 66–82.

CHAPTER 2

1. See James L. Sundquist, *Politics and Policy* (Washington, D.C.: Brookings Institution, 1968) for a narrative of political influence on policy for the 1952–66 period.

2. Barbara Hinckley, *Stability and Change in Congress*, 2nd ed. (New York: Harper and Row, 1978), ch. 6.

3. Frank J. Sorauf, *Party Politics in America* (Boston: Little, Brown, 1968), 381.

4. Aage Clausen, *How Congressmen Decide: A Policy Focus* (New York: St. Martin's Press, 1973), pp. 104–116. For an update of the Clausen study see Aage Clausen and Carl Van Horn "The Congressional Response to a Decade of Change: 1963–1972," *Journal of Politics* 39 (Aug. 1977):624–66.

5. Barbara Deckard Sinclair, "Party Realignment and the Transformation of the Political Agenda: The House of Representatives, 1925–1938," *American Political Science Review* 71 (Sept. 1977):940–53.

6. See Steiner, *The State of Welfare*, 138–43 for a discussion of changes in housing policy which followed the 1948 election. Also see Sundquist, *Politics and Policy*, for the effect of the 1964 election on policy.

7. Sundquist, *Politics and Policy*, 471–81.

8. Randall B. Ripley, *Majority Party Leadership in Congress* (Boston: Little, Brown, 1969); Charles O. Jones, *The Minority Party in Congress* (Boston: Little, Brown, 1970).

9. Barry Bozeman, "Effects of Economic and Partisan Change on Federal Appropriations," *Western Political Quarterly* 30 (March 1977):112–24.

10. Otto A. Davis, M.A.H. Dempster, and Aaron Wildavsky, "Toward a Predictive Theory of Government Expenditures: U.S. Domestic Appropriations," *British Journal of Political Science* 4 (Oct. 1974):419–452, esp. p. 431. See also, Otto A. Davis, M.A.H. Dempster, and Aaron Wildavsky, "A Theory of the Budgetary Process," *American Political Science Review* 60 (Sept. 1966):529–47; Otto A. Davis, M.A.H. Dempster, and Aaron Wildavsky, "On the Process of Budgeting: An Empirical Study of Congressional Appropriations," *Papers in Non-market Decision Making I* (1966):63–132; Otto A. Davis, M.A.H. Dempster, and Aaron Wildavsky, "On the Process of Budgeting II: An Empirical Study of Congressional Appropriation," ch. 9 in *Studies in Budgeting*, ed. R.F. Byrne et al. (Amsterdam: North Holland, 1971).

11. Clausen, *How Congressmen Decide*, 104–16.

12. Barbara Deckard Sinclair, "The Policy Consequences of Party Realignment—Social Welfare Legislation in the House of Representatives, 1933–54," *American Journal of Political Science* 22 (Feb. 1978):83–105, esp. p. 95.

13. Clausen, *How Congressmen Decide*, 90.

14. Joseph Cooper and Gary Bombardier, "Presidential Leadership and Party Success," *Journal of Politics* 30 (Nov. 1968):1012–27.

15. Barbara Hinckley, "Coalitions in Congress: Size in a Series of Games," *American Politics Quarterly* 1 (July 1973):339–59. Also see Barbara Deckard Sinclair, "Political Upheaval and Congressional Voting: The Effects of the 1960's on Voting Patterns in the House of Representatives," *Journal of Politics* 38 (May 1976):326–45.

16. Barry R. Weingast, "A Rational Choice Perspective on Congressional Norms," *American Journal of Political Science* 23 (May 1979):245–62; and Kenneth A. Shepsle and Barry R. Weingast, "Political Preferences for the Pork Barrel: A Generalization," *American Journal of Political Science* 25 (Feb. 1981):96–111.

17. E.E. Schattschneider, *Party Government* (New York: Holt, Rinehart, and Winston, 1942).

18. Accounts of legislative efforts of Truman, Kennedy, and especially Johnson emphasize presidential arm twisting and presidential favors. See, for example, Roland Evans and Robert Novak, *Lyndon B. Johnson: The Exercise of Power* (New York: New American Library, 1966). Also George C. Edwards III, *Presidential Influence in Congress* (San Francisco: Freeman, 1980).

19. Thomas Cronin, *The State of the Presidency.* 2nd ed. (Boston: Little, Brown, 1980).

20. Charles E. Lindblom, *The Policy-Making Process.* 2nd ed. (Englewood Cliffs, N.J.: Prentice-Hall, 1980), 60.

21. Samuel P. Huntington, "Congressional Responses to the Twentieth Century," in *The Congress and America's Future*, ed. David B. Truman (Englewood Cliffs, N.J.: Prentice-Hall, 1965):5–31.

22. Sundquist, *Politics and Policy.*

23. Gary Orfield, *Congress and Social Change* (New York: Harcourt Brace Jovanovich, 1975).

24. Paul C. Light, The President's Agenda (Baltimore: Johns Hopkins Univ. Press, 1982).

25. Edwards, *Presidential Influence in Congress.*

26. Douglas A. Hibbs, Jr., "Political Parties and Macroeconomic Policy," *American Political Science Review* 71 (Dec. 1977):1467–87.

27. Nathaniel Beck, "Parties, Administrations, and American

Macroeconomic Outcomes," *American Political Science Review* 76 (March 1982):83–93.

28. Douglas A. Hibbs, Jr., "Comment on Beck," *American Political Science Review* 77 (March 1983):135–38; Nathaniel Beck, "Comment on Hibbs," *American Political Science Review* 78 (June 1984):499–502.

29. Edward Tufte, *Political Control of the Economy* (Princeton: Princeton Univ. Press, 1978).

30. Ibid., ch. 1.

31. John H. Kessel, "The Parameters of Presidential Politics," *Social Science Quarterly* 55 (June 1974):8–24.

32. Bruno S. Frey and Friedrich Schneider, "An Empirical Study of Politico-Economic Interaction in the United States," *Review of Economics and Statistics* 60 (May 1978):174–83; also see Bruno S. Frey, *Modern Political Economy* (New York: Wiley, 1978).

33. Frey and Schneider, "An Empirical Study of Politico-Economic Interaction," 180–81.

34. David G. Golden and James M. Poterba, "The Price of Popularity: The Political Business Cycle Reexamined," *American Journal of Political Science* 24 (Nov. 1980):696–714.

35. Richard F. Winters and Joel Reidenberg, "Appropriations Politics and the Political Business Cycle," (manuscript, Dartmouth College), 23.

36. Ibid., and D. Roderick Kiewiet and Mathew McCubbins, "Appropriations Decisions as a Bilaterial Bargaining Game Between President and Congress," *Legislative Studies Quarterly* 10 (1985) 181–202 do include congressional variables in their analysis of agency appropriations.

37. Ripley, *Majority Party Leadership*, 168.

38. Clinton Rossiter, *The American Presidency* (New York: Mentor Books, 1960), 50–51.

39. Martha Derthick, *Policymaking for Social Security*, 342.

40. Tufte, *Political Control of the Economy*.

41. John Manley, *The Politics of Finance* (Boston: Little, Brown, 1970), 341.

42. Richard F. Fenno, Jr., *The Power of the Purse* (Boston: Little, Brown, 1966), 360–61.

43. Davis, Dempster, and Wildavsky, "Toward a Predictive Theory," 431.

44. Glenn Parker and Suzanne Parker, "Factions in Committees: The U.S. House of Representatives," *American Political Science Review* 73 (March 1979):85–102.

45. See U.S. Executive Office of the President, Office of Management and Budget, "Sensitivity of Federal Expenditures to Unemployment," Technical Paper Series, April 18, 1980.

46. This was also one of the important findings of the comparative state politics literature. For a summary of the findings of these studies see Richard I. Hofferbert, "State and Community Policy Studies," in *Political Science Annual* 3, ed. James A. Robinson (Indianapolis: Bobbs-Merrill, 1972), 3–72.

47. Robert Jackman, *Politics and Social Equality: A Comparative Analysis* (New York: Wiley, 1975).

48. Phillip Cutright, "Political Structure, Economic Development, and National Social Security Programs," *American Journal of Sociology* 70 (March 1965):537–50.

49. Jackman, *Politics and Social Equality*, 203.

50. Henry Aaron, "Social Security: International Comparisons" in *Studies in the Economics of Income Maintenance*, ed. Otto Eckstein (Washington, D.C.: Brookings Institution, 1967), 13–48.

51. Harold L. Wilensky, *The Welfare State and Equality* (Berkeley: Univ. of California Press, 1975).

52. B. Guy Peters, "Social Change, Change and Public Policy: A Test of a Model" in *Dynamics of Public Policy*, ed. Richard Rose (New York: Sage, 1977), 113–56.

53. Arnold J. Heidenheimer, Hugh Heclo, and Carolyn Adams, *Comparative Public Policy* (New York: St. Martin's, 1975), 190. Used with permission. © 1975 by St. Martin's Press, Inc.

54. The series used in this study does not include private transfers or state social welfare expenditures. The exclusion of these expenditures understates the total social welfare effort in the United States. A more comprehensive measure of social welfare effort has been developed by OECD. When comparisons are made between nations using this measure, "GNP shares are in general substantially larger and inter-country differences are less pronounced." See Jurgen Kohl, "Trends and Problems in Postwar Public Expenditure Development in Western Europe and North America" in *The Development of Welfare State in Europe and America*, ed. Peter Flora and Arnold J. Heidenheimer (New Brunswick: Transaction Books, 1981), 307–44 and esp. p. 318. State and local expenditures have been excluded since we are interested in the federal social welfare effort. Allowing the responsibility for social welfare to remain with the states, rather than being assumed by the federal government, is, in part, a political decision which may be reflected in party differences and party control.

55. William Nordhaus, "The Political Business Cycle: An Empirical Test," *Review of Economic Studies* 42 (April 1975):169–

89; C. Duncan MacRae, "A Political Model of the Business Cycle," *Journal of Political Economy* 85 (April 1977):239–63; see also, James E. Alt and K. Alec Chrystal, *Political Economics* (Berkeley: Univ. of California Press, 1983); Tufte, *Political Control of the Economy.*

56. Tufte, *Political Control of the Economy,* 57.

57. Frey and Schneider, "An Empirical Study of Politico-Economic Interaction."

58. Golden and Poterba, "The Price of Popularity."

59. Tufte, *Political Control of the Economy,* 43.

60. Gilbert Y. Steiner, *Social Insecurity* (Chicago: Rand McNally, 1966).

61. David R. Mayhew, *Congress: The Electoral Connection* (New Haven: Yale Univ. Press, 1974); Morris P. Fiorina, *Congress: Keystone of the Washington Establishment* (New Haven: Yale Univ. Press, 1977); R. Douglas Arnold, *Congress and the Bureaucracy* (New Haven: Yale Univ. Press, 1979).

62. Douglas Cater, *Power in Washington* (New York: Random House, 1964); Theodore Lowi, "How the Farmers Get What They Want," *The Reporter* (May 21, 1964):34–37; Joel Aberbach, "Bureaucrats and Clientele Groups: A View From Capitol Hill," *American Journal of Political Science* 22 (Nov. 1978):818–32; Lawrence Dodd and Richard Schott, *Congress and the Administrative State* (New York: Wiley, 1979); Arnold, *Congress and the Bureaucracy.*

63. Moynihan, *The Politics of a Guaranteed Income.*

64. Fenno, *The Power of the Purse;* Aaron Wildavsky, *The Politics of the Budgetary Process,* 2nd ed. (Boston: Little, Brown, 1974). See also Ira Sharkansky, "Agency Requests, Gubernatorial Support and Budget Success in State Legislatures," *American Political Science Review* 62 (Dec. 1968):1220–31.

65. Fenno, *The Power of the Purse;* Stephen Horn, *Unused Power: The Work of the Senate Committee on Appropriations* (Washington, D.C.: Brookings Institution, 1970); Manley, *The Politics of Finance.*

66. Derthick, *Policymaking for Social Security;* Moynihan, *The Politics of a Guaranteed Income;* M. Kenneth Bowler, *The Nixon Guaranteed Income Proposal* (Cambridge, Mass.: Ballinger, 1974).

67. David E. Price, *Who Makes the Laws* (Cambridge, Mass.: Schenkman, 1972). For a thorough analysis of committee studies, see the review essay by Heinz Eulau and Vera McCluggage, "Standing Committees in Legislatures: Three Decades of Research," *Legislative Studies Quarterly* 9 (May 1984):195–270.

68. Richard F. Fenno, Jr. *Congressmen in Committees* (Boston: Little, Brown, 1973).

69. Ibid., ch. 3.

70. Ibid., 207–209.

71. Fenno, *The Power of the Purse*, and Manley, *The Politics of Finance.*

72. Fenno, *Congressmen in Committees*, p. 209.

73. Theodore J. Lowi, "American Business, Public Policy, Case-Studies, and Political Theory," *World Politics* 16 (July 1964):677–715.

74. Fenno, *Congressmen in Committees*, 228–29.

75. Fenno, *Congressmen in Committees.*

76. John Manley, "The Family Assistance Plan: An Essay on Incremental and Nonincremental Policy-Making" in 1970 paper quoted in Moynihan, *The Politics of a Guaranteed Income*, 10.

77. Hinckley, *Stability and Change in Congress*, ch. 5.

CHAPTER 3

1. See the discussion in Thomas Dye, *Politics, Economics, and the Public: Policy Outcomes in the American States* (Chicago: Rand McNally, 1966); see Jesse F. Marquette and Katherine A. Hinckley, "Views Through a Kaleidoscope: The Dimensions of State Welfare Policy Measures," *Western Political Quarterly* 36 (Sept. 1983):466–78 for a discussion and analysis of policy measures used in the comparative state politics literature.

2. Admittedly, this policy model is drawn simply and recursively. We have omitted any feedback of outcomes and impacts on political and economic influences. The focus here is limited to emphasize the measurement of policy at each step in the process. With the policy measurement clarified, we can then specify the relationships more clearly.

3. See studies which Bruno Frey, in *Modern Political Economy* (New York: Wiley, 1978), terms politico-economic models. These studies consider a limited range of political institutional explanations.

4. Fenno, *The Power of the Purse.*

5. Peter Natchez and Irwin Bupp, "Policy and Priority in the Budgetary Process," *American Political Science Review* 67 (Sept. 1973):951–63; George C. Edwards III and Ira Sharkansky, "Executive and Legislative Budgeting: Decision Routines for Agency Totals and Individual Programs in Two States" in *Perspectives on Public Policy Making*, ed. William Gwyn and George C. Edwards III (New Orleans: Tulane Studies in Political Science, 1975).

6. Allen Schick, "How the Budget Was Won and Lost" in

President and Congress: Assessing Reagan's First Year, ed. Norman J. Ornstein, 14–43, esp. p. 34 (Washington, D.C.: American Enterprise Institute, 1982).

7. Congressional Quarterly, *Budgeting for America* (Washington, D.C., 1982), 47–54; *U.S. Budget, FY83,* 6:32. (Washington, D.C.: Government Printing Office, 1982).

8. Fenno, *The Power of the Purse,* p. xxvii.

9. Martha Derthick, *Uncontrollable Spending for Social Service Grants* (Washington, D.C.: Brookings Institution, 1975).

10. *U.S. Budget, 1971,* 42.

11. *U.S. Budget, 1985* (Washington, D.C.: Government Printing Office, 1984), 2:22.

12. Schick, "How the Budget Was Won and Lost," 26.

13. David A. Braybrooke and Charles Lindblom, *A Strategy of Decision* (New York: Free Press, 1963); George C. Edwards III and Ira Sharkansky, *The Policy Predicament* (San Francisco: Freeman, 1978), ch. 9. John Bailey and Robert O'Connor, "Operationalizing Incrementalism: Measuring the Muddles," *Public Administration Review* 35 (Jan.–Feb. 1975):60–66; Lance T. LeLoup, "The Myth of Incrementalism: Analytical Choices in Budgetary Theory," *Polity* 10 (Summer 1978):488–509.

14. Robert Albritton, "Measuring Public Policy: Impacts of the Supplemental Security Income Program," *American Journal of Political Science* 23 (Aug. 1979):559–79; Bowler, *The Nixon Guaranteed Income Proposal.*

15. Steiner, *The State of Welfare,* ch. 2.

16. Moynihan, *The Politics of a Guaranteed Income,* see also Paul Schulman, "Nonincremental Policy Making: Notes Toward an Alternative Paradigm," *American Political Science Review* 69 (Dec. 1975):1354–70.

17. Arnold J. Heidenheimer, Hugh Heclo, and Carolyn Teich Adams, *Comparative Public Policy,* 2nd ed. (New York: St. Martin's, 1983), 212. Used with permission. © 1983, St. Martin's Press, Inc.

18. Robert X Browning, "Presidents, Congress, and Policy Outcomes: U.S. Social Welfare Expenditures, 1949–1977," *American Journal of Political Science* 29 (May 1985): 197–216, reprinted by permission of the University of Texas Press; Greg A. Caldeira and Andrew T. Cowart, "Budgets, Institutions, and Change: Criminal Justice Policy in America," *American Journal of Political Science* 24 (Aug. 1980): 413–38.

19. Davis, Dempster, and Wildavsky, "Toward a Predictive Theory of Government Expenditures," 4 (Oct. 1974):419–52, esp. p. 431.

20. See also the critical comments on the Davis, Dempster, and Wildavsky model in John Wanat, "Bases of Budgetary Incrementalism," *American Political Science Review* 68 (Sept. 1974):1221–28; and John F. Padgett, "Bounded Rationality in Budgetary Research," *American Political Science Review* 74 (June 1980):354–72; Gregory W. Fischer and Mark S. Kamlet, "Explaining Presidential Priorities: The Competing Aspiration Levels Model of Macrobudgeting Decision Making." *American Political Science Review* 78 (June 1984):356–371.

21. Valerie Bunce, "Changing Leaders and Changing Policies: The Impact of Elite Succession on Budgetary Priorities in Democratic Countries," *American Journal of Political Science* 24 (Aug. 1980), 391.

22. U.S. Executive Office of the President, Office of Management and Budget, *Special Analysis A, FY83* (Washington, D.C.: Government Printing Office, 1982), 4:5.

23. Allen Schick, *Congress and Money* (Washington, D.C.: Urban Institute, 1980), 261–64; Schick, "How the Budget Was Won and Lost," 31–32.

24. Expenditures for all uncontrollable payments to individuals in 1981 were 4 percent higher than previous year estimates. For health programs, the expenditures were 10 percent higher than estimates. See *U.S. Budget, FY83*, 6:32.

25. Schick, *Congress and Money*, p. 32, observes, "The Appropriations Committees do not take action with regard to the amounts expended in a given year. Rather they provide authority to obligate funds, with much of the outlay occurring in later years. As a result, a cut in appropriations rarely is matched dollar for dollar by a reduction in outlays. Depending on the spending rate of the program, it might take as much as a $5 billion cut in budget authority to achieve a $1 billion reduction in outlays during the budget year."

26. All are effective dates of indexation.

27. Nordhaus, "The Political Business Cycle," 169–89; MacRae, "A Political Model of the Business Cycle," 239–63; see also Alt and Chrystal, *Political Economics.*

28. Hibbs, "Political Parties and Macroeconomic Policy," 1467–87; Tufte, *Political Control of the Economy.*

29. Frey and Schneider, "An Empirical Study of Politico-Economic Interaction, 174–83; also see Frey, *Modern Political Economy;* Golden and Poterba, "The Price of Popularity," 696–714.

30. Bozeman, "Effects of Economic and Partisan Change on Federal Appropriations," 112–24.

31. Caldeira and Cowart, "Budgets, Institutions, and Change."

CHAPTER 4

1. Fenno, *The Power of the Purse;* Bozeman, "Effects of Economic and Partisan Change on Federal Appropriations," 112–24; and Kiewiet and McCubbins, "Appropriations Decisions as a Bilateral Bargaining Game Between President and Congress," all base their analysis on agencies and bureaus. These analyses tend to exclude the programs included here.

2. Sharkansky, "Agency Requests, Gubernatorial Support and Budget Success in State Legislatures," 1220–31.

3. Programs move between sections of the budget with disturbing frequency for any researcher following an agency or program across time. One cannot assume that the same programs are within the same agencies or functional category from year to year.

4. U.S. Congressional Research Service, "Major Human Resource Programs: Summary and Analysis of Program and Funding Changes; FY 1970 to FY 1984," Rept. no. 83-77 EPW (March 25, 1983).

5. U.S. Executive Office of the President, Office of Management and Budget *1983 Catalog of Federal Domestic Assistance* (Washington, D.C.: Government Printing Office, 1984), iv. The *CFDA* has been published since 1965. The publication originated under the auspices of the Office of Economic Opportunity as an effort to apprise individuals, governments, and organizations of available federal programs.

6. See U.S. Department of Health, Education, and Welfare, Social Security Administration, Office of Research and Statistics, *Social Welfare Expenditures under Public Programs in the United States, 1929–66.* See also annual updates in issues of the *Social Security Bulletin* and the data in the *Annual Statistical Supplement* to the *Bulletin.*

7. This series was published annually in *CQ Almanac* through 1974.

8. David Price, "Policy Making in Congressional Committees," *American Political Science Review* 72 (June 1978):548–74; Barbara Hinckley, "Policy Content, Committee Membership, and Behavior," *American Journal of Political Science* 36 (May 1974):433–441; Fenno, *Congressmen in Committees;* Parker and Parker, "Factions in Committees," 85–102.

9. Plotnick and Skidmore, *Progress Against Poverty;* Levitan and Taggart, *The Promise of Greatness.*

10. Hofferbert, "State and Community Policy Studies," 3–72.

11. See U.S. Executive Office of the President, "Sensitivity of Federal Expenditures to Unemployment."

12. Clausen, *How Congressmen Decide*, 104–16; Clausen and Van Horn, "The Congressional Response to a Decade of Change," 624–66.

13. Lowi, "American Business, Public Policy, Case-Studies, and Political Theory," 677–715; Randall B. Ripley and Grace A. Franklin, *Congress, The Bureaucracy, and Public Policy*, rev. ed. (Homewood, Ill.: Dorsey Press, 1980); Gerald Strom, "Congressional Policy Making: A Test of a Theory," *Journal of Politics* 37 (Aug. 1975):711–35.

14. The functional budget categories are detailed in the U.S. budget documents. For further background see Executive Office of the President, Office of Management and the Budget, "The Functional Classification in the Budget," Technical Paper Series (rev. Feb. 22, 1979).

15. Although the OMB publishes functional category data for some previous years in the back of the annual budget, these data are not comparable with functional category data found in previous year budgets because of the changes within functional and subfunctional categories. Data must be adjusted for comparability. The presidential recommendations and outlays were collected from the annual budgets. Outlays were also obtained as a separate series from the Office of Management and Budget.

16. Plotnick and Skidmore, *Progress Against Poverty*; and Robert D. Plotnick, "Social Welfare Expenditures and the Poor: The 1965–1976 Experience and Future Expectations," *Policy Analysis* 5 (Summer 1979):271–90.

17. See Plotnick, "Social Welfare Expenditures and the Poor," and *Special Analysis of the Budget*.

18. *The Special Analysis of the Budget* is published annually with the executive budget. During the 1970s the analysis of income security expenditures shows benefits accruing to different beneficiary groups.

19. The SSA series was used in previous analyses. Browning, "Presidents, Congress, and Policy Outcomes.

20. *U.S. Budget 1976*, 135.

21. See Henry Aaron, *Politics and the Professors* (Washington, D.C.: Brookings Institution, 1978) for a discussion of the different approaches to combating poverty underlying Great Society Programs.

22. Calculations from 1977 Social Security Administration data.

23. See Steiner, *The State of Welfare*, ch. 7.

CHAPTER 5

1. All real dollars are deflated by a fiscal year deflator for personal consumption expenditures for the years 1950–1976 and by the calendar year deflator after that when the fiscal calendar changes (1972 = 100).

2. All of the years referred to in this chapter are fiscal years. The convention we use is to refer to the fiscal year by the year which it ends. FY50 runs from July 1, 1949 to June 30, 1950. Beginning with FY77, the fiscal year runs from October 1 to September 30.

3. The figures in Tables 5-2 and 5-3 show that there is very little difference when the SSA social welfare series data and the budget social welfare data are used. In the balance of the chapter, the budget data are relied upon since they are complete for the Carter and Reagan administrations. The averages for presidential administrations will be computed on the basis of four-year terms. As Tables 5-2 and 5-3 reveal, this decision makes little difference and allows the periods to be seen more distinctly.

4. The growth rates for the Reagan administration use estimates for fiscal 1985.

5. It should be noted that it is possible for positive and negative new budget authority to cancel each other in the same year or across years. Expansions possible under existing authority do not show up in this category either. The child nutrition programs were often expanded under existing authority. Reductions of existing authority show up negatively under new authority.

6. Requests are calculated as the percentage difference of estimated outlays over actual outlays of the previous fiscal year. This percentage change figure shows what the president estimated spending would be over what it was in the previous fiscal year. The precise figure for previous year outlays is not actually known at the time the president's budget is compiled, but an estimated figure is known. Inspection reveals very little difference between actual outlays (published two years later) and the estimated outlays (published one year later). This base reflects the changes Congress made in the budget and the economic conditions of that year. The president's proposed outlays represent requested changes plus his estimates of economic conditions for the current year. The actual percentage changes are based on changes in actual outlays in the current fiscal year over the previous fiscal year.

7. *U.S. Budget 1985*, 2:21.

8. Ratio is actual outlays divided by outlays requested by the president.

9. Public assistance programs were, until the enactment of Supplemental Security Income (SSI), federal and state programs. The growth in this category was influenced by what the states spent. AFDC remains a federal-state program, but is a smaller share of total public assistance benefits.

10. U.S. Government Accounting Office. "What Can Be Done to Check the Growth of Federal Entitlement and Indexed Spending?" (March 3, 1981), 10.

11. *U.S. Budget 1985*, 6:32.

12. GAO terms food stamps an entitlement; the Congressional Research Service does not; Schick terms it a *de facto* entitlement.

13. U.S. Government Accounting Office. "What Can Be Done to Check the Growth of Federal Entitlement and Indexed Spending?," 12.

14. This means that the appropriation is for a definite amount appropriated annually.

15. *U.S. Budget 1985*, 2:21.

CHAPTER 6

1. U.S. Executive Office of the President, Office of Management and Budget, *Payments For Individuals, 1985 Budget* (Washington, D.C., 1984), p. 1.

2. Veterans education benefits have been removed from payments to students. They have a cycle of their own, which differs from the other student assistance programs.

3. The interaction term is the number of House nonsouthern Democrats times the presidential dummy variable. Since this variable is equal to 0 during Republican administrations, the interaction term is an extra effect of the number of House nonsouthern Democrats during Democratic presidencies which is hypothesized to stimulate social spending.

4. During the Nixon administration in-kind programs grew. Coding the Nixon administration as a Democratic administration overestimates spending; coding it as a Republican understates it. It is left coded as Republican. The coding change making Carter a Republican changes the R^2 from 0.17 to 0.56. This effect is not observed with cash expenditures.

CHAPTER 7

1. For a history of the development of the Social Security Act, see Witte, *The Development of the Social Security Act*.

2. Altmeyer, *The Formative Years of Social Security.*

3. For a history of changes and issues in social security, see Derthick, *Policymaking for Social Security.*

4. Ibid., ch. 4.

5. Ibid., ch. 13.

6. See *Congress and the Nation I* (Washington, D.C.: Congressional Quarterly, 1965), p. 1252, relating HEW Secretary Arthur Flemming's comments to the Senate Finance Committee on Aug. 8, 1978.

7. Martha Derthick, "How Easy Social Security Votes Came to an End," *Public Interest* 39 (Winter 1979):94–105.

8. Tufte, *Political Control of the Economy.*

9. For changes in public assistance provisions, see Steiner, *The State of Welfare*, chs. 1–3.

10. See Steiner, *Social Insecurity.*

11. Moynihan, *The Politics of a Guaranteed Income.*

12. See *Social Security Bulletin, Annual Statistical Supplement* for current and past provisions of the matching formula and other conditions.

13. See Steiner, *The State of Welfare*, ch. 6; Maurice MacDonald, *Food, Stamps and Income Maintenance* (New York: Academic Press, 1977); U.S. Congress, Congressional Budget Office, "The Food Stamp Program: Income or Food Supplementation?" Budget Issue Paper (Washington, D.C.: Government Printing Office), Jan. 1977.

14. Randall B. Ripley, "Legislative Bargaining and the Food Stamp Act, 1964" in *Congress and Urban Problems*, ed. Frederic N. Cleaveland, et al., 279–310 (Washington, D.C.: Brookings Institution, 1969).

15. "The Food Stamp Program: Income or Food Supplementation?," 7.

16. U.S. Congress, Senate, Committee on the Budget, *Indexation of Federal Programs*, prepared by Congressional Research Service (May 1981), 15.

17. Veterans' pensions are essentially welfare benefits paid to war time veterans who qualify based on age, income, and a "nonservice connected" disability. Compensation benefits are based on service connected death or disability.

18. See Steiner, *The State of Welfare*, ch. 7.

19. See Derthick, *Policymaking for Social Security*, ch. 17.

20. Manley, *The Politics of Finance.*

21. Ibid., 202–3.

22. See Derthick, *Policymaking for Social Security*, 350.

23. Derthick's account of the changes in the system made in 1972 is one of the best descriptions of the positions of the major actors. See ibid., 350–62.

24. U.S. Senate, *Indexation of Federal Programs*, 15.

CHAPTER 8

1. Levitan and Taggart also make this point in *The Promise of Greatness*.

2. William Greider, *The Education of David Stockman and Other Americans* (New York: Dutton, 1981), 153.

3. Ibid., 155–56.

4. Congressional Quarterly, *Budgeting for America*, 102–3.

5. Ibid., 99.

6. John L. Palmer and Isabel V. Sawhill, *The Reagan Experiment* (Washington, D.C.: Urban Institute, 1982); John L. Palmer and Isabel V. Sawhill eds., *The Reagan Record* (Washington, D.C.: Urban Institute, 1984); Lester M. Salamon and Michael S. Lund, eds. *The Reagan Presidency and the Governing of America* (Washington, D.C.: Urban Institute, 1984).

7. Plotnick, "Social Welfare Expenditures and the Poor," 271–90.

8. Ibid., 26.

9. See Page, *Who Gets What From Government*, 91–94.

Bibliography

Aaron, Henry. "Social Security: International Comparisons" in
  Studies in the Economics of Income Maintenance, ed. Otto
  Eckstein, pp. 13–48. Washington, D.C.: Brookings Institution,
  1967.
———. *"Politics and the Professors.* Washington, D.C.: Brookings
  Institution, 1978.
Aberbach, Joel. "Bureaucrats and Clientele Groups: A View From
  Capitol Hill." *American Journal of Political Science* 22 (Nov.
  1978):818–32.
Albritton, Robert. "Measuring Public Policy: Impacts of the
  Supplemental Security Income Program." *American Journal of
  Political Science* 23 (Aug. 1979):559–79.
Alt, James A., and K. Alec Chrystal. *Political Economics.* Berkeley:
  Univ. of California Press, 1983.
Altmeyer, Arthur J. *The Formative Years of Social Security.* Madison:
  Univ. of Wisconsin Press, 1966.
Anderson, Martin. *Welfare.* Stanford, Calif.: Hoover Institution
  Press, 1978.
Arnold, R. Douglas. *Congress and the Bureaucracy.* New Haven: Yale
  Univ. Press, 1979.
Bailey, John, and Robert O'Connor. "Operationalizing
  Incrementalism: Measuring the Muddles." *Public
  Administration Review* 35 (Jan.–Feb. 1975):60–66.
Barth, Michael C., George J. Carcagno, and John L. Palmer. *Toward an
  Effective Income Support System: Problems, Prospects and
  Choices.* Madison, Wisc.: Institute for Research on Poverty,
  1974.
Beck, Nathaniel. "Parties, Administrations, and American
  Macroeconomic Outcomes." *American Political Science
  Review* 76 (March 1982):83–93.

————. "Comment on Hibbs." *American Political Science Review* 78 (June 1984):499–502.

Bixby, Ann Kallman. "Social Welfare Expenditures, Fiscal Year 1980," *Social Security Bulletin* 46 (Aug. 1983):9–17.

Bowler, M. Kenneth. *The Nixon Guaranteed Income Proposal.* Cambridge, Mass.: Ballinger, 1974.

Bozeman, Barry. "Effects of Economic and Partisan Change on Federal Appropriations." *Western Political Quarterly* 30 (March 1977):112–24.

Browning, Robert X. "Presidents, Congress, and Policy Outcomes: U.S. Social Welfare Expenditures, 1949–1977." *American Journal of Political Science* 29 (May 1985):197–216.

Braybrooke, David A., and Charles Lindblom. *A Strategy of Decision.* New York: Free Press, 1963.

Bunce, Valerie. "Changing Leaders and Changing Policies: The Impact of Elite Succession on Budgetary Priorities in Democratic Countries." *American Journal of Political Science* 24 (Aug. 1980):373–95.

Caldeira, Greg A., and Andrew T. Cowart. "Budgets, Institutions, and Change: Criminal Justice Policy in America." *American Journal of Political Science* 24 (Aug. 1980):413–38.

Cater, Douglas. *Power in Washington.* New York: Random House, 1964.

Clausen, Aage. *How Congressmen Decide: A Policy Focus.* New York: St. Martin's Press, 1973.

Clausen, Aage, and Carl Van Horn. "The Congressional Response to a Decade of Change: 1963–1972." *Journal of Politics* 39 (Aug. 1977):624–66.

Congressional Quarterly. *Budgeting for America.* Washington, D.C.: Congressional Quarterly, 1982.

————. *Congress and the Nation.* Washington, D.C.: Congressional Quarterly, 1965.

Cooper, Joseph, and Gary Bombardier. "Presidential Leadership and Party Success." *Journal of Politics* 30 (Nov. 1968):1012–27.

Cronin, Thomas. *The State of the Presidency.* 2nd ed. Boston: Little, Brown, 1980.

Cutright, Phillip. "Political Structure, Economic Development, and National Social Security Programs." *American Journal of Sociology* 70 (March 1965):537–50.

Danziger, Sheldon, and Robert Plotnick. "The War on Income Poverty: Achievements and Failures" in *Welfare Reform in America*, ed. Paul M. Sommers (Boston: Kluwer-Nijhoff Publishing, 1982), pp. 31–52.

Davis, Otto A., M.A.H. Dempster, and Aaron Wildavsky. "Toward a Predictive Theory of Government Expenditures: U.S. Domestic Appropriations." *British Journal of Political Science* 4 (Oct. 1974):419–52.

_____. "A Theory of the Budgetary Process." *American Political Science Review* 60 (Sept. 1966):529–47.

_____. "On the Process of Budgeting: An Empirical Study of Congressional Appropriations." *Papers in Non-market Decision Making I* (1966):63–132.

_____. "On the Process of Budgeting II: An Empirical Study of Congressional Appropriation." Ch. 9 in *Studies in Budgeting*, ed. R.F. Byrne et al. Amsterdam: North Holland, 1971.

Derthick, Martha. *Policymaking for Social Security.* Washington, D.C.: Brookings Institution, 1979.

_____. *Uncontrollable Spending for Social Service Grants.* Washington, D.C.: Brookings Institution, 1975.

_____. "How Easy Social Security Votes Came to an End." *Public Interest* 39 (Winter 1979):94–105.

Dodd, Lawrence, and Richard Schott. *Congress and the Administrative State.* New York: Wiley, 1979.

Dye, Thomas. *Politics, Economics, and the Public: Policy Outcomes in the American States.* Chicago: Rand McNally, 1966.

Edwards, George C. III. *Presidential Influence in Congress.* San Francisco: Freeman, 1980.

Edwards, George C. III, and Ira Sharkansky. "Executive and Legislative Budgeting: Decision Routines for Agency Totals and Individual Programs in Two States" in *Perspectives on Public Policy Making*, ed. William Gwyn and George C. Edwards III. New Orleans: Tulane Studies in Political Science, 1975.

_____. *The Policy Predicament* (San Francisco: Freeman, 1978).

Eulau, Heinz, and Vera McCluggage, "Standing Committees in Legislatures: Three Decades of Research," *Legislative Studies Quarterly* 9 (May 1984):195–270.

Evans, Roland, and Robert Novak. *Lyndon B. Johnson: The Exercise of Power.* New York: New American Library, 1966.

Fenno, Richard F. Jr. *The Power of the Purse*. Boston: Little, Brown, 1966.

———. *Congressmen in Committees*. Boston: Little, Brown, 1973.

Fiorina, Morris P. *Congress: Keystone of the Washington Establishment*. New Haven: Yale Univ. Press, 1977.

Fischer, Gregory W., and Mark S. Kamlet, "Explaining Presidential Priorities: The Competing Aspiration Levels Model of Macrobudgeting Decision Making." *American Political Science Review* 78 (June 1984):356–71.

Frey, Bruno S. *Modern Political Economy*. New York: Wiley, 1978.

Frey, Bruno S., and Friedrich Schneider. "An Empirical Study of Politico-Economic Interaction in the United States." *The Review of Economics and Statistics* 60 (May 1978): 174–83.

Garfinkel, Irwin, and Robert Haveman. "Income Transfer Policy in the United States: A Review and Assessment," Discussion Paper #701-82. Madison, Wisc: Institute for Research on Poverty, 1982.

Golden, David G., and James M. Poterba. "The Price of Popularity: The Political Business Cycle Reexamined." *American Journal of Political Science* 24 (Nov. 1980):696–714.

Greider, William. *The Education of David Stockman and Other Americans*. New York: Dutton, 1981.

Haveman, Robert H., ed. *A Decade of Federal Antipoverty Programs*. New York: Academic Press, 1977.

Heidenheimer, Arnold J., Hugh Heclo, and Carolyn Adams. *Comparative Public Policy*. New York: St. Martin's, 1975; 2nd ed., 1983.

Hibbs, Douglas A. Jr. "Political Parties and Macroeconomic Policy." *American Political Science Review* 71 (Dec. 1977):1467–87.

———. "Comment on Beck." *American Political Science Review* 77 (March 1983):135–38.

Hinckley, Barbara. *Stability and Change in Congress*. 2nd ed. New York: Harper and Row, 1978.

———. "Coalitions in Congress: Size in a Series of Games." *American Politics Quarterly* 1 (July 1973):339–59.

———. "Policy Content, Committee Membership, and Behavior." *American Journal of Political Science* 36 (May 1974):433–41.

Hofferbert, Richard I. "State and Community Policy Studies" in

Political Science Annual 3:3–72, ed. James A. Robinson. Indianapolis: Bobbs-Merrill, 1972.

Horn, Stephen. *Unused Power: The Work of the Senate Committee on Appropriations.* Washington, D.C.: Brookings Institution, 1970).

Huntington, Samuel P. "Congressional Responses to the Twentieth Century" in *The Congress and America's Future,* ed. David B. Truman, pp. 5–31. Englewood Cliffs, N.J.: Prentice-Hall, 1965.

Jackman, Robert. *Politics and Social Equality: A Comparative Analysis.* New York: Wiley, 1975.

Jones, Charles O. *The Minority Party in Congress.* Boston: Little, Brown, 1970.

Kessel, John H. "The Parameters of Presidential Politics," *Social Science Quarterly* 55 (June 1974):8–24.

_____. *The Domestic Presidency: Decision Making in the White House.* North Scituate, Mass: Duxbury Press, 1975.

Kiewiet, D. Roderick, and Mathew D. McCubbins. "Appropriations Decisions as a Bilateral Bargaining Game Between President and Congress," *Legislative Studies Quarterly* 10 (1985):181–202.

Kohl, Jurgen. "Trends and Problems in Postwar Public Expenditure Development in Western Europe and North America" in *The Development of Welfare State in Europe and America,* ed. Peter Flora and Arnold J. Heidenheimer, 307–44. New Brunswick: Transaction Books, 1981.

Lampman, Robert. *Ends and Means of Reducing Income Poverty.* New York: Academic Press, 1971.

_____. "What Does it Do for the Poor? A New Test for National Policy." *Public Interest* 34 (Winter 1974):66–82.

LeLoup, Lance T. "The Myth of Incrementalism: Analytical Choices in Budgetary Theory." *Polity* 10 (Summer 1978):488–509.

Levitan, Sar A. *Programs in Aid of the Poor.* 4th ed. Baltimore: Johns Hopkins Univ. Press, 1980.

Levitan, Sar, and Robert Taggart. *The Promise of Greatness.* Cambridge, Mass.: Harvard Univ. Press, 1976.

Light, Paul C. *The President's Agenda.* Baltimore: Johns Hopkins Univ. Press, 1982.

Lindblom, Charles E. *The Policy-Making Process.* 2nd ed. Englewood Cliffs, N.J.: Prentice Hall, 1980.

Lowi, Theodore. "American Business, Public Policy, Case-Studies, and Political Theory." *World Politics* 16 (July 1964):677–714.

——. "How the Farmers Get What They Want." *The Reporter* (May 21, 1964):34–37.

MacDonald, Maurice. *Food, Stamps and Income Maintenance.* New York: Academic Press, 1977.

McMillan, Alma, and Ann Kallman Bixby. "Social Welfare Expenditures,Fiscal Year 1978." *Social Security Bulletin* 43 (May 1980):3–17.

MacRae, C. Duncan. "A Political Model of the Business Cycle." *Journal of Political Economy* 85 (April 1977):239–63.

Manley, John. *The Politics of Finance.* Boston: Little, Brown, 1970.

Marquette, Jesse F., and Katherine A. Hinckley. "Views Through a Kaleidoscope: The Dimensions of State Welfare Policy Measures." *Western Political Quarterly* 36 (Sept. 1983):466–78.

Mayhew, David R. *Congress: The Electoral Connection.* New Haven: Yale Univ. Press, 1974.

Moynihan, Daniel P. *The Politics of a Guaranteed Income.* New York: Vintage Books, 1973.

Natchez, Peter, and Irwin Bupp. "Policy and Priority in the Budgetary Process." *American Political Science Review* 67 (Sept. 1973):951–63.

Nordhaus, William. "The Political Business Cycle: An Empirical Test." *Review of Economic Studies* 42 (April 1975):169–89.

Orfield, Gary. *Congress and Social Change.* New York: Harcourt Brace Jovanovich, 1975.

Padgett, John F. "Bounded Rationality in Budgetary Research." *American Political Science Review* 74 (June 1980):354–72.

Page, Benjamin I. *Who Gets What from Government.* Berkeley: Univ. of California Press, 1983.

Palmer, John L., and Isabel V. Sawhill, eds. *The Reagan Experiment.* Washington, D.C.: Urban Institute, 1982.

——, eds. *The Reagan Record,* Washington, D.C.: Urban Institute, 1984.

Parker, Glenn, and Suzanne Parker. "Factions in Committees: The U.S. House of Representatives." *American Political Science Review* 73 (March 1979):85–102.

Patterson, James T. *America's Struggle Against Poverty 1900–1980.* Cambridge, Mass.: Harvard Univ. Press, 1981.

Peters, B. Guy. "Social Change, Change and Public Policy: A Test of a Model." 113–56 in *Dynamics of Public Policy*. Ed. Richard Rose. New York: Sage, 1977.

Plotnick, Robert D. "Social Welfare Expenditures and the Poor: The 1965–1976 Experience and Future Expectations." *Policy Analysis* 5 (Summer 1979):271–90.

_____ and Felicity Skidmore. *Progress Against Poverty*. New York: Academic Press, 1975.

Price, David. "Policy Making in Congressional Committees." *American Political Science Review* 72 (June 1978):548–74.

Price, David E. *Who Makes the Laws*. Cambridge, Mass.: Schenkman, 1972.

Ripley, Randall B. *Majority Party Leadership in Congress*. Boston: Little, Brown, 1969.

_____. "Legislative Bargaining and the Food Stamp Act, 1964" in *Congress and Urban Problems*, ed. Frederic N. Cleaveland, et al., pp. 279–310. Washington, D.C.: Brookings Institution, 1969.

Ripley, Randall B., and Grace A. Franklin. *Congress, The Bureaucracy, and Public Policy*. Rev. ed. Homewood, Ill.: Dorsey Press, 1980.

Robinson, James A. *Congress and Foreign-Policy Making*. Homewood, Ill.: The Dorsey Press, 1967.

_____, ed. *Political Science Annual* 3 (Indianapolis: Bobbs-Merrill, 1972).

Rossiter, Clinton. *The American Presidency*. New York: Mentor Books, 1960.

Schattschneider, E.E. *Party Government*. New York: Holt, Rinehart, and Winston, 1942.

Salamon, Lester M., and Michael Lund, eds. *The Reagan Presidency and the Governing of America* (Washington, D.C.: Urban Institute Press, 1984).

Schick, Allen. *Congress and Money*. Washington, D.C.: Urban Institute, 1980.

_____. "How the Budget Was Won and Lost" in *President and Congress: Assessing Reagan's First Year*, ed. Norman J. Ornstein. Washington, D.C.: American Enterprise Institute, 1982, pp. 14–43.

Schulman, Paul. "Nonincremental Policy Making: Notes Toward an

Alternative Paradigm." *American Political Science Review* 69 (Dec. 1975):1354–70.

Sharkansky, Ira. "Agency Requests, Gubernatorial Support and Budget Success in State Legislatures." *American Political Science Review* 62 (Dec. 1968):1220–31.

Shepsle, Kenneth A., and Barry R. Weingast. "Political Preferences for the Pork Barrel: A Generalization." *American Journal of Political Science* 25 (Feb. 1981):96–111.

Sinclair, Barbara Deckard. "The Policy Consequences of Party Realignment—Social Welfare Legislation in the House of Representatives, 1933–54." *American Journal of Political Science* 22 (Feb. 1978):83–105.

————. "Political Upheaval and Congressional Voting: The Effects of the 1960's on Voting Patterns in the House of Representatives." *Journal of Politics* 38 (May 1976):326–45.

————. "Party Realignment and the Transformation of the Political Agenda: The House of Representatives, 1925–1938." *American Political Science Review* 71 (Sept. 1977):940–53.

Sommers, Paul M., ed. *Welfare Reform in America.* Boston: Kluwer-Nijhoff, 1982.

Sorauf, Frank J. *Party Politics in America.* Boston: Little, Brown, 1968.

Steiner, Gilbert Y. *Social Insecurity.* Chicago: Rand McNally, 1966.

————. *The State of Welfare.* Washington, D.C.: Brookings Institution, 1971.

Gerald Strom, "Congressional Policy Making: A Test of a Theory," *Journal of Politics* 37 (Aug. 1975):711–35.

Strom, Gerald. "Congressional Policy Making: A Test of a Theory," *Journal of Politics* 37 (Aug. 1975):711–35.

Sundquist, James L. *Politics and Policy.* Washington, D.C.: Brookings Institution, 1968.

Tufte, Edward. *Political Control of the Economy.* Princeton: Princeton Univ. Press, 1978.

U.S. Congress. Congressional Budget Office. "The Food Stamp Program: Income or Food Supplementation?" Budget Issue Paper. Washington, D.C.: Government Printing Office, Jan. 1977.

————. Senate. Committee on the Budget. *Indexation of Federal*

Programs, prepared by Congressional Research Service, 97th Congress, 1st session, May 1981.

U.S. Congressional Research Service. "Major Human Resource Programs: Summary and Analysis of Program and Funding Changes; FY 1970 to FY 1984." Rept. no. 83-77 EPW (March 25, 1983).

U.S. Department of Health, Education and Welfare. Social Security Administration. Office of Research and Statistics. *Social Welfare Expenditures under Public Programs in the United States, 1929–66,* Research Report no. 25. Washington, D.C. Government Printing Office, 1968.

U.S. Executive Office of the President, Office of Management and Budget. *Report on Indexing Federal Programs.* Washington, D.C. Government Printing Office, 1981.

———. *The Budget of the United States Government, Fiscal Year,* various years. Washington, D.C. Government Printing Office, 1981, 1984.

———. "Sensitivity of Federal Expenditures to Unemployment." Technical Paper Series, April 18, 1980.

———. "The Functional Classification in the Budget." Technical Paper Series, rev. Feb. 22, 1979.

———. *Payments for Individuals, 1985 Budget.* Washington, D.C., 1984.

———. *1983 Catalog of Federal Domestic Assistance,* Washington, D.C.: Government Printing Office, 1984.

———. *Special Analysis A, FY83.* Washington, D.C.: Government Printing Office, 1982.

U.S. Government Accounting Office. "What Can Be Done to Check the Growth of Federal Entitlement and Indexed Spending?" (March 3, 1981).

U.S. Joint Economic Committee. *Studies in Public Welfare,* Paper no. 2, "Handbook of Public Income Transfer Programs" 92nd Congress, 2nd Session, Oct. 16, 1972.

Wanat, John. "Bases of Budgetary Incrementalism." *American Political Science Review* 68 (Sept. 1974):1221–28.

Weingast, Barry R. "A Rational Choice Perspective on Congressional Norms." *American Journal of Political Science* 23 (May 1979):245–62.

Wildavsky, Aaron. *The Politics of the Budgetary Process.* 2nd ed.
    1974; 3rd ed. Boston: Little, Brown, 1979.
Wilensky, Harold L. *The Welfare State and Equality.* Berkeley: Univ.
    of California Press, 1975.
Winters, Richard F., and Joel Reidenberg. "Appropriations Politics
    and the Political Business Cycle" (manuscript, Dartmouth
    College).
Witte, Edwin E. *The Development of the Social Security Act.*
    Madison: Univ. of Wisconsin Press, 1963.

Index

Politics and Social Welfare Policy in the United States was composed into type on the Mergenthaler Linotron 202N Phototypesetter in ten point Trump Medieval with three points of spacing between the lines. The book was designed by Sheila Hart, typeset by The Composing Room of Michigan, Inc., printed offset by Thomson-Shore, Inc., and bound by John H. Dekker & Sons. The paper on which the book is printed is designed for an effective life of at least three hundred years.

THE UNIVERSITY OF TENNESSEE PRESS : KNOXVILLE